ELIZABETH GRIFFIN

ABOUT THE AUTHORS

ANDREA LAVINTHAL is a beauty editor in New York City. She feels about twenty-five—until she has to leave a bar because it's too crowded, too loud, or filled with too many actual twenty-five-year-olds.

JESSICA ROZLER works in book publishing in New York City. Most days, she feels like she is twenty-five. On those mornings when Jessica is nursing a hangover, however, she feels about as old as Yoda, but without all of the wisdom.

Your So-Called Life

Also by Andrea Lavinthal and Jessica Rozler

FRIEND OR FRENEMY?

THE HOOKUP HANDBOOK

Your So-Called Life

A Guide to Boys, Body Issues, and Other Big-Girl Drama
You Thought You Would Have Figured Out by Now

Andrea Lavinthal and
Jessica Rozler

HARPER

NEW YORK · LONDON · TORONTO · SYDNEY

HARPER

HarperCollins books may be purchased for educational, business, or sales
promotional use. For information please write: Special Markets Department,
HarperCollins Publishers, 10 East 53rd Street, New York, NY 10022.

FIRST HARPER EDITION PUBLISHED 2010.

Designed by Ruth Lee-Mui

Library of Congress Cataloging-in-Publication Data is available upon request.

ISBN 978-0-06-193838-2

10 11 12 13 14 OV/RRD 10 9 8 7 6 5 4 3 2 1

Contents

Part III: Bonus Features:
You're All Grows Up, So Deal with It
233

Introduction

It's Only Natural: Puberty, Part Deux
(a.k.a Your So-Called Life or Redo-berty)

Jeremy: Someday you'll look back on all this and laugh, say we
              were young and stupid.
John: We're not that young.

—from *Wedding Crashers*

LET'S HAVE some girl talk. Now that you're growing up, you might notice some, um, changes in your body. Don't be embarrassed—it's nothing to be ashamed of. You're just experiencing a time of transition, like when a moth emerges from a cocoon or a bubblegum teen queen poses for provocative magazine photos because she wants to prove to the world that she's not that innocent.

Yes, your hormones are raging, hair is appearing in places it never has before, and that indeed is a pimple on your forehead. And on your chin. And on your back. (But fear not. It's nothing the Proactiv three-step acne management system can't fix. Just ask Katy Perry, Avril Lavigne, or whichever celeb is currently hawking the zit zapper.) Anyway, all of these changes are part of becoming a woman. That being said, happy ~~thirteenth~~ thirtieth birthday!

Welcome to coming of age, the sequel—or, as we like to call it, your so-called life (an homage to one of the best television shows ever) or redo-berty (get it?). Yep, it's the dirty little secret that the school nurse neglected to mention in her frank discussions about hair down there, your monthly cycle, and other things that are "only natural."

Just when you thought you left your wonder years behind, hidden away in a box in your parents' attic along with your Judy Blume books and cheerleading bloomers, you reach a certain age that really gets you thinking about what it means to be an adult. This life reevaluation often happens at some point in your late twenties to early thirties (with the big 3-0 serving as a milestone birthday), long after you squirmed your way through a litany of firsts (first period, first bra, first kiss) and Electric Slided while a deejay with a terrible name like "Blaze" or "Krush" spun tunes in honor of your bat mitzvah, confirmation, sweet sixteen, *quinceañera*, or any of the other rites of passage that prematurely solidified your "adult" status.

Unlike physical adolescence, this re–coming of age is all about blossoming into a genuine twenty-four-karat big girl and dealing with all of the emotional and psychological changes that accompany it. It's also a time of contradictions. Maybe you've advanced in the working world, but you feel like you've fallen behind in your personal life. Or you're on point when it comes to personal matters, but you've derailed off of the career track.

During redo-berty, you're also old enough to experience the consequences of choices made in youngish adulthood (those years during college and right after where you played with your newfound freedom), and the resulting dissatisfaction, uncertainty, or—if shit really hits the fan—upheaval can make you feel like you're going through another puberty. (And, for the record, the *P* word still grosses us out as much as it did back during those days of talks with the aforementioned school nurse, which is why we're sticking with redo-berty or your so-called life.)

And, nope, these puberty-like pangs of angst aren't the so-called quarterlife crisis, a post-college moment of clarity when you finally realized that working at a job actually requires, you know, *work*, and your BA in Russian poetry (with a minor in pottery) was total BS.

You're twenty-two and feeling indignant because your big bad fashion editor boss wants you to go to Starbucks and get her an extra-hot nonfat half-caf latte? Boohoo. Cry us a river.

Actually, in all seriousness, we should give credit where credit is due. Even though we've all heard about the quarterlife crisis, here's some more background about this post-college breakdown: Authors Alexandra Robbins and Abby Wilner brought the term into the national lexicon with their 2001 book, which was aptly named *Quarterlife Crisis: The Unique Challenges of Life in Your Twenties*. In it, they describe the feelings of indecision, helplessness, instability, anxiety, fear, and a host of other not-so-good-stuff that hit people in their twenties after they leave the structure of formal education and venture out into the often overwhelming world of endless choices.

Robbins and Wilner write: "The extreme uncertainty that twenty-somethings experience after graduation occurs because what was once a solid line that they could follow throughout their series of education institutions has now disintegrated into millions of different options. The sheer number of possibilities can certainly inspire hope—that is why people say that twentysomethings have their whole lives ahead of them. But the endless array of decisions can make a recent graduate feel utterly lost."

The authors also note that a quarterlife crisis can rear its ugly head in a different way—especially during your mid- to late twenties. Life or work isn't giving you the fulfillment you expected, and you feel disappointed and ask questions like "Is this all there is?" (Which is kind of like how we felt after watching the series finale of *The Sopranos*.)

Robbins and Wilner broke some serious ground with their tome. However, we think that the lesser-known definition of the quarterlife crisis—those feelings that hit in your later twenties and into your thirties—warrants its own book. That being said, the redo-berty years can be thought of as kinda sorta the tail end of the quarterlife crisis. You dig? It's when stuff starts getting serious. You've already experienced your early twenties, when it was OK not to have things figured out. Now, it's game time, and the real maturation begins— hence these puberty-like feelings.

So, in case you missed it, here's a rundown: Your so-called life is the Rest-of-Your-Life Crisis, the beginning of the seventy-five percent of your time on this planet that isn't sponsored by American Apparel. And, as you move toward your real adult years, you start asking yourself the kind of deep, philosophical questions that can send even the sanest of women to a therapist, like, What is my purpose? Can I really have it all? And, am I too over-the-hill to be watching *The Hills*? This is also a time when you realize that *someday* is actually *today*, *tomorrow* is really *tomorrow* instead of the distant future, and the future only belongs to the future itself . . . and the future is Electric Youth! (Thanks for clearing that last part up for us, Debbie—sorry, *Deborah*—Gibson.)

Crisis Control: Puberty, the Quarterlife Crisis, and Redo-berty

By now you should realize that—like shoulder pads and jumpsuits— feelings of angst and uncertainty aren't safely hidden in the past. They come back into style, often when you least expect them to. And just in case you're having trouble keeping your awkward phases straight, here, in handy chart form, is a breakdown of your breakdowns.

	Puberty	**Quarterlife Crisis**	**Redo-berty**
Age range	For girls, approximately 9 through 16; for boys, approximately 13 through 45	Technically 21 to 30 (but most people think of it as those few years right after college)	26 to 34
Monumental birthday	13	25	30
Defining moment	Menses	Transitioning from watching *The Real World* to living in "the real world," which in no way resembles the TV show	Buying your own place, or at the very least getting a couch that doesn't come with assembly instructions
Major misconceptions about age	That 20 is old	That 30 is old	That any age is old
A great big lie that adults told you about relationships	Boys seldom make passes at girls who wear glasses.	He's just not that into you.	You always find someone when you're not looking. (If this were the case, Match.com and JDate wouldn't be so successful.)

	Puberty	Quarterlife Crisis	Redo-berty
What's going on down there?	A strange new tingly sensation whenever Mr. Paul, the hottie student teacher in history class, stands near your desk	A lot of pulling and praying (you must have not been paying attention in health class)	An episiotomy
Britney song that sums up everything	"I'm Not a Girl, Not Yet a Woman"	"Oops! . . . I Did It Again"	"My Prerogative" (And yes, we're aware that *Bahhhhhhhby!!!!* Brown first recorded this song.)
Fashion fail	Neon colors and leggings	Pink velour tracksuit with Uggs . . . and a trucker hat	Neon colors and leggings the second time around
Your object of lust	Mr. Paul, your hottie student teacher in history class, who kinda sorta looks like Luke Perry	Ramon, the hunky head of the eco-volunteer program where you are working hard in the rainforests of Costa Rica to (continued)	Chris, the fresh-faced intern at work, who kinda sorta looks like a younger Luke Perry (you cougar, you)

	Puberty	**Quarterlife Crisis**	**Redo-berty**
Your object of lust (continued)		save tropical fire ants that fart oxygen into the atmosphere	
Motto	"I must, I must, I must increase my bust!"	"That's hot." (Barf!!!)	"If you liked it, then you shoulda put a ring on it."
Mortifying moment	Wearing white jeans when you receive a surprise visit from Aunt Flo (wink, wink) in the middle of science lab	Resorting to a McJob right after you graduate from school (FYI: You're still too stuck in your self-important college phase to realize that this isn't actually a "mortifying moment." It's "reality" since —surprise, surprise—BAs in Russian poetry don't exactly bring home the bank.)	Having to move back in with your parents

	Puberty	Quarterlife Crisis	Redo-berty
Scary ailment	Cooties	Herpes	Cankles
Must-have beauty product	Stridex pads	Deodorant stone	Eye cream
Home away from home	The food court at the mall	Your friendly neighborhood pub (They have a happy hour that lasts from 4 p.m. to 8 p.m. every day and one of those Photohunt machines. Believe us— you'd want to live there, too.)	What do you mean? I'm *nesting* right now.
Relationship status	You + Joey from NKOTB 4-Eva	Single and ready to mingle (You ditched the college BF after realizing that he was actually serious about becoming a musician.)	Spooning on the couch with your SO/DH (which stand for "significant other" and "dear husband," for those of you who haven't yet been schooled in the ways of (continued)

	Puberty	**Quarterlife Crisis**	**Redo-berty**
Relationship status (continued)			shmoopy woopy couples' shorthand)
Lofty goal for the future	Save the princess in *Super Mario Bros.*	Save the world	Save enough money to put granite countertops in the kitchen

Things in your life are changing at a lightning-fast pace, or perhaps you feel like everyone around you is growing up and you're going to be left if their dust. (Just a note: The redo-berty phenomenon tends to hit at a later age if you live in a big urban area.) Mortgages, careers, layoffs, marriages, divorces, families, financial crises, aging parents, biological clocks—welcome to Big-Girl-Ville, population: you.

It also doesn't help that adulthood is different than it used to be. This ain't your mother's 30, 26, 34, 28, (or whatever your current age), meaning there are no hard-and-fast rules about where you're supposed to be in your life right now. On one hand, the freedom is great, but on the other, it's extremely terrifying.

And this brings up a question of our own: Even though it's normal, *why* do we experience this profound reevaluation? And, even more important, why *now*? OK, those were two questions. We have more choices than previous generations had, and thankfully, most of us don't need to toil away in dangerous, backbreaking jobs in order to put food on the table or stay home and raise a brood of children when we've barely left childhood behind ourselves. Haven't we planned and studied and interned so that we don't ever have to experience uncertainty? If so, then why are we feeling so lost?

Enter Kevin Brennan, Psy.D, who, from here on, will be known as "Dr. Kevin." Dr. Kevin is a licensed clinical psychologist concentrating on Young Professional issues. Throughout this book, he'll be offering up some insight into life during the redo-berty years. To backtrack for a moment, Dr. Kevin sees patients who struggle with what we commonly know as quarterlife crises (or QLCs, for short), but they tend to be older than the just-out-of-college crowd. Basically, the redo-berty years are part of his definition of the quarterlife crisis. (To-MAY-to, to-MAH-to, right?)

"The term 'quarterlife' as I know it professionally is somewhat different than the public view of the term. While it tends to bring up ideas of a twenty-five-year-old, I often see that the problems of quarterlife more harshly affect men and women in their late twenties and early thirties," he says.

Dr. Kevin goes on to explain why we're feeling the crunch at this later age. "Why now? Because they have been able to put off adulthood for an impressively long time, and it's getting to be time to pay the piper. The concrete is beginning to set," he says. "The heaviness around their ankles is made up of jobs that are turning into careers, student loans that can no longer be put off, relationships that turn from 'fun' to 'serious,' women turning from 'girls' to 'moms,' or similarly, from 'girls' to 'women whose baby-time is nearing an end,' and generally more and more responsibilities and commitments are being presented that make them feel like real adults for the first time in their whole lives."

Another possible (and surprising) reason that we're experiencing growing pains the second time around is this: because we can. With more opportunity comes more pressure to have it all: the HGTV-worthy house (screw the two-bedroom starter dumphole—doesn't every grown-up need at least five bedrooms and four bathrooms, not to mention a water feature in the backyard?); the perfect significant other (your sexy, supportive soul mate who knows how to dress and, like, totally isn't gay); the adorable kiddies (nothing says "success" like an $800 stroller); and don't forget about the fulfilling yet well-paying job that you can leave at 5 p.m. every night and get home early enough to enjoy the house, the well-dressed significant other who totally isn't gay, the perfect kids, and the water feature. Now, we're not suggesting that our expanded menu of choices is a bad thing. We're all for freedom and variety, and we still prefer a choose-you-own-adventure story to a boring and formulaic plot, *thankyouverymuch*. It's just that we need manage our expectations and stop being so hard on ourselves. We can't have it all. Well, Kelly Ripa is an exception. How does she do it?

After all, the idea that we have to follow our passions or we'll die inside is also a relatively new phenomenon. (Remember, this isn't your mother's thirty.)

"Our parents didn't have time to think about 'what they wanted out of life,'" Dr. Kevin says. "They were not afforded options to feel out what would be best for them."

Speaking of our parents, there is one possible bright spot to your so-called life. The fact is that people of our generation are getting their angst out now, which could lessen the likelihood of, or reduce the severity of, a midlife crisis. Dr. Kevin explains: "Speaking in generalizations, this generation has had privileges of time, space, and lack of responsibility that their mothers and fathers did not until their midlives. Probably, their grandparents did not ever have these privileges. What this gave our generation is ample time to ask questions of themselves that their parents generally didn't think to ask until midlife, when *they* had the time, space, and lack of responsibility."

Dr. Kevin goes on to say that we have been given the responsibility to "get life right" by a generation of people who felt they did not. They had no such pressure, nor the privilege of being able to attempt to figure it out early. By finding out what makes us happy now, we might not have to ditch the first wife for the perky receptionist at the gym or get hair plugs later on in life. Or something to that effect. "In essence, we are having our midlife crises early," notes Dr. Kevin. "Now, there may be further recapitulations of these crises in the future, but I predict nothing matching the severity of this one. We got most of it out of our system already."

That bit of good news aside, let's get back to our regularly scheduled kvetching. In addition to dealing with the pressure to live "perfect" lives and have it all, today we also have the added anxiety of living our lives more publicly than ever before, something that really contributes to the angst of the redo-berty years. Remember back in seventh grade when your friends were making out with boys behind the bleachers while you were still struggling to fill out a training bra? Now, you can log onto Facebook and find out that your sorority sister got engaged, your friend got a promotion, and your little cousin got knocked up (and it was actually planned). Thanks to social networking and other forms of digital dishing, not only can we spend hours navel-gazing online (e.g. blogging in puns about our search for Mr. Right in the big scary city), but we also can gaze at one another's navels via social networking sites. It's easier than ever to compare and contrast our friends' life trajectories to our own and then blog, tweet, text, and Gchat about it. And, sure, sharing is caring, but recent research shows that too much talk, particularly among teen girls—yes, we know you're a grown-ass woman, but lessons can still be learned here—heightens feelings of anxiousness and depression, and digital communication is intensifying this.

And, let's up the anxiety factor even more and not forget that the media doesn't exactly play fair when it comes to women and aging. Even if you're not hyperventilating about growing older or hopelessly trapped in kidulthood (by the way, Ms. Maturity, you might own a KitchenAid mixer, but we all know that you also share your twelve-year-old niece's affinity for *Glee*, Nintendo Wii, and Justin Bieber), sometimes it feels like everyone else is trying to convince you that you should be. Throughout each day, whether we're conscious of it or not, we're bombarded with conflicting messages about women and age. Lurid tales of Baby Botox, va-jay-jay rejuvenation, and collagen-enhanced cougars (oh my!) intermingle with helpful "advice" about loving yourself (at any age—and as long as you're a size four!), celebrating your impending sexual peak (because, really, isn't that the only thing that matters?), and embracing your womanhood (which sounds suspiciously like a Summer's Eve commercial). Yep, when it comes to women, age, and empowerment, our society is keeping it about as real as J.Lo did back when she tried to work that whole "Jenny from the Block" routine.

Adult acne, digital co-ruminating, and the media's sexist take on aging (*Viva Viagra!*)—no wonder we have mixed feelings about getting older. But don't forget to look on the bright side: We now have an Old Country Buffet of choices compared to the limited menu that was offered to previous generations of women. We can get married, get a promotion, see that cute guy from the party last Saturday, see the world, start a family, start a business, or any combination of the above. At the risk of sounding a little you-go-girlish, getting older has never been as empowering—or hotter—than it is right now. Think of it as a hot new trend! As of this writing, all of the Jessicas (Simpson, Alba, and Biel) and all of the Kates (Holmes, Hudson, and Bosworth) are nearing or have hit the big 3-0. Also, according to a recent study reported in *The Daily Telegraph*, the majority of women said that they felt their sexiest at thirty-four. Hey, cute yet obviously underage girl at the bar wearing a tiny, shiny camisole even though it's the middle of the winter, put that in your pipe—or roll it into your Virginia Slim—and smoke it! Also, let's not forget that with age comes confidence, wisdom, self-awareness (unless of course, you're one of the Real Housewives of Orange Country, New Jersey, or wherever), perspective, experience, and all that other good stuff. (Plus, silver hair can look pretty awesome.)

Your So-Called Life: A Guide to Boys, Body Issues, and Other Big-Girl Drama You Thought You Would Have Figured Out by Now is an über-informative guide to breaking through the awkwardness and becoming an adult during this strange time when Forever 21, Facebook, and *Guitar Hero* aren't just for kids. The book will act as a literary GPS, guiding you along the exhilarating, scary, and thrilling road trip to becoming an adult on your own terms, all while offering expert advice, a much-needed dose of nostalgia, real stories from real women, and hopefully some real giggles. It's also a look at adulthood in this newish millennium, when the rules have changed.

The redo-berty years are when *eventually* becomes *now, never,* or *will I ever?* They're also about growing up but realizing that you don't have to settle—because, after all, settling is for upset stomachs and all of those thin, pretty sitcom wives that are married to roly-poly, beer-swigging semi-lovable losers. (Gotta love primetime television!)

So, um, yeah. We thought that was some pretty inspiring feel-good talk. But judging by the look on your face, you're still feeling a bit jittery about transforming into a butterfly. Well, let's examine some of your fears and help you realize that maybe you're overreacting just a teeny tiny bit.

CALMING YOUR IRRATIONAL FEARS ABOUT GROWING UP

IRRATIONAL FEAR #1: Once you hit a certain age, your looks are going to start going downhill faster than Miley Cyrus's purity.
THE TRUTH: To our knowledge, vampires aren't real, so like every other creature on this planet, we're eventually going to die. Having

some fear about aging is only natural because getting older reminds us that we are mere mortals. And, for practical reasons, there are legitimate concerns about aging, perceptions of vitality, and the workplace. However, you can blame Hollywood and its obsession with eternal youth for any completely and utterly irrational fears about growing older—the type of hysteria that has driven millions of women, at younger and younger ages, to trade the ability to make facial expressions for foreheads that are smoother than freshly Zambonied ice. Luckily, the reality is a bit kinder and gentler. (Besides, we'll take a gorgeous silver-haired Emmylou Harris any day over a bleached-out, used-up, barely legal starlet.) We're serious. Have you looked at your sixth-, seventh-, and eighth-grade yearbook photos lately? Aqua Net–shellacked bangs? Check. Crimped hair? Check. Side ponytail? Check. Obviously, the worst is behind you when it comes to your personal styling choices, and much like fine wine, you're only gonna get better—and more deliciously complex—with age, wrinkles and all.

IRRATIONAL FEAR #2: Ohmygod, you're going to die alone.
THE TRUTH: If by "die alone," you mean that you're never going to get married, don't worry. Statistically, most of us will get hitched at some point in our lives. In fact, according to recent research by the National Center for Health Statistics, 86 percent of women are married by age forty. Keep in mind, though, that just because you exchange vows with Mr. Right and torture your BFFs with hideous bridesmaids dresses doesn't guarantee that you're going to stay married (surely you don't need to be reminded of the dismal divorce rate) or have someone to take care of you in your old age (duh, that's what children are for). Also, who says that a holy union will automatically bring you eternal bliss? Remember that Disney movie where Princess Pretty-Hair learns that she has to find happiness within herself before she can marry Prince Even-Prettier-Hair? Okay, so maybe that's not

exactly how it goes down in a land far, far away, but perhaps it should. And here's one last thing to think about: Like birth, death is a solo mission, unless you're a member of a cult where everyone counts to three and then chugs some cyanide-laced purple drink, leaving this evil world behind.

IRRATIONAL FEAR #3: You're going to lose common ground with your friends.

THE TRUTH: This is a vintage irrational fear, dating back to your tween years when you and your childhood best friend did everything together. Then, she got her period and her mother took her shopping for her first real bra, leaving you behind to practice French kissing with your pillow. When you reached your early twenties, there was a brief period of time when things evened out and most of your friends' lives mirrored your own. However, as you hit your late twenties and beyond, it seems like everyone is doing their own thing. Some people are flying solo, others have traveled to faraway lands, and others are married with 2.5 kids. (On a related note, if you're currently raising two and a half children, you should try to get featured on one of those freaky medical mystery documentaries on TLC.) Just because the members of your social circle are at different stages in life doesn't mean that you aren't going to be friends anymore. Diversity is a good thing.

IRRATIONAL FEAR #4: Your wunderkind days are over.

THE TRUTH: Hate to break it to you, Doogie Howser, but this is part of growing up. On the bright side, there are plenty of adults out there who are dazzled by simple, shiny things (which explains the popularity of *Dancing with the Stars* and Kim Kardashian). That being said, you might not be a child genius, but you can still wow 'em without actually having any talent. Plus, if you've already earned a doctorate in astrophysics, written an opus, or sold your website for millions before you graduated from college, what is there to look forward to other than early retirement? We don't know about you, but we're not interested in relocating to Florida (a.k.a. God's waiting room) anytime soon and embarking on a not-so-busy schedule filled with canasta games and early-bird dinners.

IRRATIONAL FEAR #5: You're getting too old to change careers.

THE TRUTH: Paranoid much? According to the people who keep track of these types of things, the average person can expect to have three careers in her lifetime and hold an average of fourteen jobs before her fortieth birthday. And, in case you didn't learn this from the recession, which has forced millions upon millions of people in every age group to struggle and adapt to the realities of today's working world, we'll clue you in: The days of big fat pensions and gold watches on your twenty-fifth anniversary with the company are over. So, if you've always wanted to be a teacher or a lawyer or zookeeper, just do it. It's never too late because, in this crazy thing called life, the redo-berty years aren't old. They're just young-old. And do we really need to tell you that age is only a number? Just ask Nola Ochs, who, in 2007, became the oldest person ever to receive a college degree—at the youthful age of ninety-five. Which we hear is the new sixty-five.

IRRATIONAL FEAR #6: This is the oldest you've ever been.

THE TRUTH: Well, we can't argue with this one—actually, wait a second. What about that fake ID you used when you were nineteen years old? Weren't you Natalie Meyers, age thirty-two, from Duluth, Minnesota?

IRRATIONAL FEAR #7: You're running out of time.

THE TRUTH: Again with the paranoia. This isn't 1850, when life expectancy for women ranged from thirty-five to forty years. Back then, you could probably actually perish from a bad hair day or embarrassment, rather than just feel like crawling into a hole to die. Today, you still have time to do what you've always dreamed of doing. Okay, it's not like you're going to win a gold medal in gymnastics or become a prima ballerina, so let's do a quick rewrite: You still have the time to do what you've always dreamed of doing—*within reason*.

And this last answer is the perfect segue to the heart and soul of *Your So-Called Life*. Remember that becoming an adult is like those first few weeks at the gym. You'll be achy for a bit, but in the long run, you'll get hooked on grown-up endorphins. How do we, the authors, know? Because, we're right next to you on the elliptical machine, working on our metaphorical glutes in that metaphorical gym. In fact, it's why we wrote this book. Well, that's not exactly true. Initially, we wanted to pen a tale about a girl who falls in love with a smoking hot vampire, but we didn't think anyone would read it. That left us to examine what was going on in our own lives. We both teetered on the brink of turning thirty—a monumental birthday, no matter how you feel about it. While one of us (cough, Andrea, cough) was breathing into a paper bag at the thought of crossing the threshold into a new stage of life, the other (that would be Jessica) shrugged it off as a reason to invite all of her friends to join her in consuming copious amounts of alcohol while she flitted about in a party dress (from Forever 21, by the way). Of course, that doesn't mean Jessica was any more prepared to become a big girl than Andrea was (the alcohol helped, though). After listening in on endless conversations with our peers about everything from career and family issues to romance and friendship, we realized that almost every girl—we mean *woman*—has strong feelings about life post–quarterlife crisis and especially strong feelings about turning thirty, ranging from dread, panic, and terror to self-reflection, nostalgia, and, yes, even some satisfaction. So, that brings us here. (Suck it, *Twilight*!)

We hope you find this book to be a funny yet realistic look at life post–quarterlife, as well as an antidote for your so-called life/redo-berty years. Get ready to be informed. As you make your way through these pages, you'll learn about the history of adulthood and get expert advice on everything from dating and cohabiting to climbing up the career ladder and throwing a big-girl party (complete with real plates!). You'll learn about your sexual health, your wealth, and yourself. In addition, you'll hear from women just like you, who are struggling with the trials and tribulations of adulthood.

And, if you still feel anxious about getting older, think about the alternative: um, not getting older, which means you wouldn't be alive. Pretty darn morbid, huh? Never forget that your life belongs to you, not a medical company that peddles facial fillers or a women's magazine that makes you feel bad about yourself or that yenta in the accounts payable department who constantly grills you about your love life (even though she hasn't spoken to her own husband in, like, twenty-five years). Own it. Love it. Take responsibility for yourself. Hell, wear miniskirts as long as you can rock them.

And use this book as your guide.

Ten Things You *Don't* Need to Do
by the Time You Become a Bona Fide Adult

We just told you what this book is going to be, so now let's tell you what it *won't* be: a long, eye-roll-inducing list of all of the wacky, wild, and crazy things that you should do before you hit some monumental birthday like thirty. (*Number 16: Kiss a stranger in the rain—in Paris!*) So, in the spirit of the noninclusion of said wacky "you go, girl" lists, we present you with ten things that you *don't* need to do before you're all grown up:

1. Go to rehab.
2. Battle it out on national television for the affections of some psuedo-celebrity.
3. Baby Botox your face until you look like a wax version of yourself.
4. Star in a sex tape that "leaks" to the Internet.
5. Get a tattoo of a butterfly, a fairy, or a dolphin on your lower back. (It's *sooo* 1994, anyway.)
6. Go bungee jumping (also *sooo* 1994).
7. Flash your ta-tas to a bunch of drunk, horny tools in exchange for a string of plastic Mardi Gras beads.
8. Make out with a girl in front of a bunch of drunk, horny tools in exchange for a round of drinks.
9. Spend a month's salary on a pair of shoes that hurt your feet.
10. Watch the entire *Sex and the City* DVD collection in one day. (*Sooo* 2004.)

Part I

GPS for Your So-Called Life:

How Did You Get Here and Where Are You Going?

In order to know where we're going, we have to know where we came from—or some shit like that. Anyway, think of this part of the book as our version of The History Channel, minus the programming on World War II, signs of the apocalypse, and the truth behind *The Da Vinci Code*. Here, we take a look at the changing face of adulthood, from Before the Common Era to the present TMI Era, a time when our life choices are endless and we feel the need to write about it all over Facebook and Twitter. (@everyone-in-the-freaking-universe: should I choose the honey mustard, Grey Poupon, spicy mustard, chipotle mayo, or horseradish?)

One

Looking Back: The Former Face of Adulthood (You Know, Before There Was Botox and Restylane)

What is happening to our young people? They disrespect their elders, they disobey their parents, they ignore the law. They riot in the streets inflamed with wild notions. Their morals are decaying. What is to become of them?

—???

Pop quiz: Who is quoted as saying the above? Was it:
a. Andy Rooney
b. Your crotchety eighth-grade English teacher
c. Yoda
d. Plato

ACTUALLY, THIS is kind of a trick question. The O.G. deep thinker himself, Plato, is widely believed to have uttered these words in the fourth century BCE. However, that was *waaaay* before we had iPhones, Facebook, or Google, so there's really no way to verify that it happened.

Arguments about attribution aside, we use a quip about kids in a book that details the growing pains of real adulthood to make a point: Intergenerational squabbling is an age-old tradition, kind of like prostitution. Although the lyrics might change with the times, the song remains the same. The elders think the young'uns are selfish and amoral slutbags, hell-bent on polluting society, while the

young'uns think the elders are stodgy old squares, hell-bent on suck-
ing the fun out of life. This battle is probably because, as the years
go by, adults tend to forget the agony and ecstasy of growing up, and
younger peeps often lack the life experience and self-awareness to
recognize their moments of foolishness. Remember when you were
too immature to realize that spandex bicycle shorts plus a skirt did
not equal a cute look? Oh, the follies of youth! OK, to be fair, there
are plenty of older selfish and amoral slutbags (see GOSSELIN, JON;
or pretty much anyone else on a reality television show, with the
WOODS, TIGER; and JAMES, JESSE), and there are certainly younger
squares (see PHILLIPS, JENNY, that tattletale who cried to her mother
that you dipped her fingers in warm water to make her pee when she
fell asleep early during a slumber party in seventh grade), but that's
a whole other book.

As you move into your redo-berty years, you'll find yourself trapped
between two worlds—the elders and the young'uns. On one hand,
you'll be the recipient of condescending advice from certain members
of the older generation who accidentally-on-purpose forgot what life
was like during the transition period to adulthood. Sure, growing up
happened a lot earlier in decades past because options were limited
compared to the multitude of choices we have today. These elders
will insist that they seamlessly and stoically made the jump to big-kid
status and all of its big-kid responsibilities, and they'll offer up varia-
tions on the old line "When I was your age, I had to walk ten miles
in the snow to get to school." ("When I was your age, I had three
kids and a house, and I didn't think twice about it.") That might be
partially true, but they still experienced self-doubt, fear, anxiety, and
the excitement of growing up for real, and if you don't believe us, you
obviously never watched *Mad Men*. It's just that this anxiety and fear
wasn't as public as it is now, and often, it manifested itself later on in

the form of midlife crisis. (For more information on digital communication and its effects on your so-called life, check out Chapter 3.)

Some old'uns might go so far as to insist that you're not actually a grown-up unless you're married with children, and they'll prod you to "get on with it" or "settle down" to match expectations of adulthood that are left over from their generation.

On the other hand, you might catch yourself slipping into the role of an elder. You'll shake your head at that girl in the mall who must have been raised by wolves—and very slutty wolves, at that—because no mother in her right mind would let her young daughter leave the house rocking microscopic jean shorts a la Daisy Duke and a full face of makeup a la *What Ever Happened to Baby Jane?* You'll fear for our future when *Time* magazine runs yet another alarmist story about whatever awful thing kids are supposedly doing these days. (What's with all of these middle schoolers "sexting" and, um, sexing? When we were that age, we either steered clear of the boys because we didn't want to get cooties, or we were preoccupied with more pressing matters like teasing our bangs and singing Madonna songs into a hairbrush while we danced around our bedrooms.) You'll feel moments of panic as a younger generation comes up and does things differently than you did. All of this is only natural—just like our favorite word, "puberty."

We guess what we're trying to say is that even though the face of adulthood is morphing thanks to our wider variety of options in life, some things never change. There will always be the angst about growing up, the Peter Pans (and the Wendys who love them), the Holden Caulfields, the rock 'n' rollers, and the late bloomers.

Now, let's look at some events throughout history that affected the how, when, and why we grow up.

THE EVOLUTION OF ADULTHOOD:
A SEMIRECENT HISTORY OF GROWN-UP MILESTONES
(YEAH, WE'RE FOCUSING ON WOMEN)

THE THIRD AND FOURTH CENTURIES BCE: While classical Greece hardly constitutes semirecent history, we wanted to throw this one in here for our man Plato. For obvious reasons (duh, the absence of Google), learning the average life expectancy in the days of Zeus proves to be a difficult task, but it is believed that most people didn't make it past forty years of age. (Plato must have taken good care of himself because lived to about eighty years young.) Knowing the short life expectancy of the ancient Greeks, we imagine the wild younger generation that was admonished in the opening quote of this chapter as a bunch of unruly eight- to ten-year-olds, drunk off wine and defacing Doric columns as they roamed the streets in depraved mobs—kind of like A Clockwork Orange, only with toga-clad grade schoolers.

To put things in perspective, a girl who lived during this time period married off around age fourteen or fifteen, and wasn't considered a true woman, or—stifle your giggles—a true *gyne*, until she had her first child. (Girls and women were classified by sexual maturity and marital status. "*Kore*" referred to prepubescents; a *parthenos* was an unmarried virgin who had already gotten her period; a married woman who hadn't had a kid yet got labeled as a *nymphe*; and married moms took the *gyne* label. Yet for some reason, "You Make Me Feel Like a Natural Gyne" doesn't have the same ring to it.)

OTHER DAYS OF YORE: We know, we know. This still isn't considered semirecent history, but we wanted to show you that you don't have things so bad if you, say, have a crappy job or a nonexistent love life. For example, according to the book *Women in Early America: Struggle, Survival, and Freedom in a New World*, by Dorothy A. Mays, in the seventeenth century, the average life expectancy for women was slightly less than forty-two years, with maternal death during child-birth playing a big role in shortening the life. Also according to the book, the average age of marriage for the ladies in colonial America was twenty-two (later than we would have guessed), with a woman expecting to go through her first bout of labor about sixteen months after saying "I do" or "Yea." Forget the honeymoon, because, typically, she would give birth every fifteen to twenty months during her next twenty years of life. Which sounds absolutely exhausting to us.

1893: While we assume that Cleopatra and her posse had some sort of garment for lifting and separating their twins, it isn't until the late 1800s that Marie Tucek patents the "breast supporter," the earliest known version of the modern-day bra. Sadly, there is no documentation of the first mother to take her daughter shopping for a training bra to support those "mosquito bites."

1913: Ella Flagg Young, superintendent of Chicago public schools, introduces a pioneering "sexual hygiene" program to students at the junior and senior high school level. According to editor Carolyn Cocca, in her book, *Adolescent Sexuality: A Historical Handbook and Guide*, Young "enlisted physicians to give lectures in students, separated by sex and matched with a medical doctor of the same sex. Lectures covered physiology, hygienic and moral advice about sexuality and behavior, and sex-related social problems, such as venereal disease." Compared to today's standards, these classes were probably as racy as an episode of *Murder, She Wrote*, but talking about sex and other unmentionables rattled the chains of concerned citizens, who eventually derailed the program. In 1915, two Michigan high school teachers introduced a "sex ed" model that has withstood the test of time: The girls go into one classroom where a female teacher talks about the wonders of menstruation, and the boys go into another classroom where the PE teacher explains that nocturnal emissions are very normal.

1929: Dr. Earle Haas, of Denver, Colorado, invents and patents the modern tampon, but he later sells the rights for his creation to Gertrude Tendrich, the woman who later becomes the first president of Tampax. Tampax makes tampons commercially available, eventually producing that icky commercial where a woman stops up a leaky boat with a Tampax Pearl (which, we must admit, is the Rolex of feminine hygiene products).

1938: Judy Blume (née Sussman) is born in Elizabeth, New Jersey. Thirty-two years later she writes the coming-of-age classic *Are You There God? It's Me, Margaret*, which covers all of the crucial topics for prepubescent girls: periods (we still don't understand how those pink sanitary belts worked), boys, and boobs.

1960: The FDA approves the use of oral contraceptives, almost fifty years after Planned Parenthood founder Margaret Sanger first started pushing for the development of a "magic pill" that would prevent pregnancy. In a curious role reversal, gender "equality" doesn't come until nearly forty years later, when the FDA approves a magic pill for men called Viagra. While the little blue wonder drug is hardly a contraceptive, Bob Dole serves as an early celebrity spokesman for the erectile wonder drug, which grosses people out so much that they don't want to have sex, thus indirectly serving as a way to prevent unwanted pregnancy.

1970: The Boston Women's Health Book Collective publishes *Our Bodies, Ourselves*, a comprehensive guide to women's health and sexuality that featured *very* detailed sketches of female genitalia. An updated version is released in 2005 with considerably less pubic hair.

1978: While most mothers try to prevent their daughters from dressing like streetwalkers ("Wipe that stuff off your face before your father comes home!"), Brooke Shields's mom actually encourages her to take the role of a preteen prostitute in the movie *Pretty Baby*. Two years later, Shields stars in *The Blue Lagoon*, a movie about a couple of shipwrecked kids who grow up together on a tropical island and get freaked out when strange things start happening "down there" because they know nothing about puberty (they missed years of sex ed, thanks to the shipwreck). Eventually, they fall in love and spend a lot of time doing it and cavorting naked on the beach, which sounds like it would be a great commercial for Sandals resorts.

1984: Congress passes the National Minimum Drinking Age Act, which raises the drinking age from eighteen to twenty-one. Canada and Mexico experience an immediate tourism boom.

1985: The first IKEA store opens in the U.S., bringing affordable yet impossible-to-assemble furniture with names that lack vowels (plus: delicious meatballs) to "adults."

1986: A *Newsweek* magazine cover story reports that if a "white, college-educated woman" hasn't married by age thirty, she might as well adopt a litter of kittens because it ain't happening. And the cherry on the "you're going to die alone" sundae is the unforgettable line that a forty-year-old single woman is "more likely to be killed by a terrorist" than to ever marry. The magazine admits "our bad" in 2006 with an article citing more recent research showing that a forty-year-old woman has a 40 percent chance of marrying.

1987: At age fifteen, Corey Feldman becomes one of the first child stars to win legal emancipation from his parents, paving the way for

Drew Barrymore, Macaulay Culkin, and, in a few years, the Gosselin children.

1987: The show *thirtysomething* debuts on ABC, highlighting the ups and downs in the lives of depressed boomers with perms.

1994: *Reality Bites* chronicles Gen-Xers as they struggle with adulthood, work at the Gap, and generally fall short of expectations. And, of course, we all cheer at the part in the movie when scuzzy, sexy Ethan Hawke and nineties screen queen Winona Ryder finally give in to their sexual tension and chew each other's faces off.

1998: Dr. Craven Kurz, the orthodontist credited with inventing invisible braces in the 1970s, passes away. For sparing grown-ass adults who weren't fortunate enough to have braces during puberty from being called "metal mouth" at age thirty-two, we salute this fine doc.

2000: Adult attention deficit hyperactivity disorder is added to the DSM-IV. If you've gotten this far in the book without stopping to send a text, check your email, comment on the pics your friend just posted on Facebook, update your Twitter page, or rewatch an episode of *Jersey Shore*, then you belong in a lab where scientists can study your superhero-like concentration.

2001: Britney Spears releases the single "I'm Not a Girl, Not Yet a Woman." In the video, she sings about her struggle between being a carefree teen and a responsible grown-up, y'all, while standing on a mountain and wearing a crop top and low-rise jeans.

2002: Botox is approved to temporarily smooth moderate to severe frown lines between the brows in people from eighteen to sixty-five years of age. Women seem happy about this, though it was difficult to tell because their faces no longer show any expression.

2004: Jennifer Garner stars in the chick flick *13 Going on 30*, which should've had the subtitle *It's Like That Movie* Big *with Tom Hanks but for Girls*. In the film, the main character wants to escape the awkwardness of girlhood and fast-forwards to when she's all grown up and "thirty, flirty, and thriving."

2006: The average age of first-time mothers increases 3.6 years since 1970, from 21.4 to 25. Jamie Lynn Spears misses the memo.

2006: Facebook expands registration beyond college students. You join, and within days, you get a flurry of friend requests from a bunch of people who are best left in the past.

2007: The very funny *Knocked Up*, starring Seth Rogan and crew, rings in the summer of the man-child, a time when men who haven't grown up yet actually think they can get Katherine Heigl in real life.

2008: The median age for marriage is the oldest since the U.S. Census started keeping track in the 1890s—almost twenty-six for women and almost twenty-eight for men.

2009: *Details* magazines reports that in a survey of a thousand British girls between the ages of fifteen and nineteen, roughly 25 percent said they aspired to become professional lap dancers, giving a whole new meaning to the question, "What do you want to be when you grow up?"

DECEMBER 21, 2012: The world is going to end. For proof, see directly above.

Intermission #2

Ten Things You *Don't* Need to Know by the Time You're a Bona Fide Adult

Hopefully, you'll gain some knowledge as you get older, but you don't need to have the answers to everything. (That's what the Internet is for.) In fact, if you ever plan on becoming a wise oracle, we're making it a little easier on you. Here are ten things that you *don't* need to know before you're a bona fide adult:

1. What you want to be when you grow up
2. The difference between shrimp and prawns
3. Whom you're going to marry (but you *should* know the difference between "who" and "whom")
4. Which one is Hall and which one is Oates
5. Your rising sign
6. Where to touch a man that will drive him wild every time (Hint: It's probably his peen.)
7. How to engage your core while in Revolved Half Moon Pose.
8. The real lyrics to "Blinded by the Light" ("Wrapped up like a douche / Another boner in the night" sounds good to us.)
9. Your future children's names (You don't want to go through all the trouble to pick out truly beautiful and creative monikers like Sparrow or Apple only to get scooped.)
10. How to make the perfect dirty martini (That's what bartenders are for.)

Two

Virtual Insanity: Your So-Called Life in the Digital Age

TRACY JORDAN: . . . You can read about that on the Interweb.

—from *30 Rock*

SOME THINGS are best left behind, like acid-washed jeans, ex-boyfriends, and grudges. However, thanks to social networking and instant everything, the past has become a thing of the past! Remember (or did you try your best to forget?) Christine Collins, the sixth-grade bully who tortured you with noogies (the middle school equivalent of waterboarding) until you handed over your lunch money? She just sent you a Facebook friend request! Or how about your stellar performance of the 4 Non Blondes's classic "What's Up?" at your high school talent show, which you hoped and prayed was safely hidden away on some long-forgotten VHS tape? Well, it's baaaack—uploaded onto YouTube for the viewing displeasure of you and a gazillion of your nearest and dearest. (Just search for your name plus "yeah, yeah, yeah" to see shaky footage of your younger self strumming an acoustic guitar and, in an unfortunate homage to the music video that accompanied the song, wearing goggles on your head and combat boots on your feet.)

In addition to letting the past become your present, social networking and digital communication give you an unprecedented glimpse into the lives of your confidantes, acquaintances, coworkers, third cousins, and virtual "friends." Every vacation, wedding, anniversary, mood, meal, playlist, and ultrasound photo is uploaded, blogged about, or made into a quiz for all to see, discuss, and envy. You no longer need to sneak glances over the picket fence to determine if the grass is indeed greener on the other side. Just log onto Facebook or whatever social network they come up with next and you can instantly see that all of your "friends" are wittier, busier, happier, and more fertile than you are, which, in turn, drives you to construct an idealized online version of yourself that will keep up with the Jones'. (OK, so you're happy for your friends, but even the most confident among us has the occasional bout of insecurity.)

Don't get us wrong. There are plenty of positive things that result from being so connected to one other. For example, Facebook offers an easy way to get back in touch with old friends and to stay in touch with the ones that live in faraway places. Plus, it enables us to have larger social networks than our parents did when they were our age. And, unlike candy corn or Christmas albums recorded by pop singers, friends are one thing that you can never have too many of.

Online social networking also lets you reveal things about yourself that you might never divulge in real life. (In case you forgot, "real life" is that thing that happens outside the confines of your computer, CrackBerry, or iPhone screen). Think of all of those online quizzes, questionnaires, and polls as getting-to-know-you games, minus the trust falls.

Of course, we can't help but let our inner Daria rear her head again. (Here comes the monotone voice. . . .) Introspection is great and all, but at what point do we go from self-reflective to self-centered? Are we spending so much time ruminating, documenting, and commentating online that we're actually stunting our growth as adults? And what about the lack of privacy and the expectation that we are available at any time? To play off of that old philosophical question about a tree falling in the forest and maybe or maybe not making a sound, if a life isn't blogged about in excruciating detail for all to read, is it actually lived?

Here's our answer: Step away from the computer. Very slowly. Now, go outside and play. Digital communication and online social networking are what you make of them. We often forget that we're in the driver's seat, and thanks to our free will, we can let that phone call go to voicemail, ignore a Facebook friend request from someone we would like to forget, and spend as little or as much time online as we damn well please. (A novel concept, isn't it?)

Overall, the good outweighs the bad when it comes to digital communication and online social networking. (And, even if the bad outweighed the good, there's no way we can stop technology from forging ahead.) Until some mad scientist perfects teleporting, sites like Facebook are a great way to share our lives—the ups, the downs, the weddings, birthdays, and babies—with the people that we wish lived across the street rather than across the country. However, nothing virtual should ever be a substitute for having real-life experiences and connections. This might sound simple enough, but it's important for all you Facebook and CrackBerry addicts out there: We need to know when to log in and when to log out and live our lives, minus the comments, the status updates, and yes, even without the cute little quizzes like "Which Care Bear Are You?" (By the way, we always thought Funshine Bear was a hot-ass bitch.)

Now, before we go any further, let's take a look at the technology of today and compare it to what we had during the good old days of youth. (How long do you give it until the cool kids start ironically sporting Zack Morris–sized cell phones?)

Au Revoir, Commadore 64:
Puberty Versus Redo-berty in the Digital Age

Puberty	Redo-berty
Passing a juicy note to your friend during social studies class	Sending a juicy email to your friend while you're at work
Getting that note you passed in social studies class intercepted by your teacher, Mr. Reed, who, by the way, isn't fooling anyone with that rug on his head	Sending a juicy email to your friend while you're at work and noticing a few seconds too late that your boss is standing behind you (Somehow you doubt that she'll think "then I gave him a BJ" is part of the presentation you're supposed to be working on.)
Nearly dying from embarrassment as Mr. Reed reads said juicy note in front of the class, revealing your lax stance on second base (You would, like, totally let Eric Nies from MTV's *The Grind* touch your boobs.)	Nearly dying from embarrassment, when you realized that you hit "reply to all" on said juicy email, revealing your lax stance on first date oral sex to your company's entire Northeast division (not that we're judging you—actually, yes, we are)
Scrawling "[Your initials] + [Your boyfriend's initials] 4-Eva" all over your binders and folders	Having your significant other in your Facebook profile photo
Signing your friend's yearbook	Writing on your friend's Facebook wall
Getting bullied	Getting cyberbullied
Keeping a diary (which, inevitably, gets read by your mother)	Keeping an anonymous blog (which, inevitably, gets picked up by *Gawker*)

Puberty	Redo-berty
Corresponding with your summer camp boyfriend via letters written on Elizabeth Arden Sunflowers–scented loose-leaf paper	Corresponding with the guy you met last summer by playing "you show me yours, I'll show you mine" on Skype (still pretending not to judge you)
Creating the perfect outgoing answering machine message featuring Bell Biv DeVoe's "Poison" (which, by the way, is still *the* jam after all these years)	Laboring a custom status message for Gchat that makes it seem like you don't really care about trying to make yourself seem cool (kind of like spending forty-five minutes to give yourself that perfect just-rolled-out-of-bed hair)
Riding your bike past the local baseball diamond because you know your crush has practice on Tuesday at 3:30	Stopping by the local sports bar because your crush just checked in via foursquare
Fighting with your friends over the free set of doubles from your after-prom party pictures	Getting mad at your friend when she uploads a photo of you with a double chin to Flickr

ADULTS THESE DAYS:
THE GOOD NEWS AND THE BAD NEWS ABOUT
THE CURRENT STATE OF DIGITAL COMMUNICATION

It's hard to remember a time when a phone call was the quickest way to get in touch with someone, newspapers were our go-to source for the latest in current events, and Lindsay Lohan dated men. Or women. Or men. Aw, forget it. It's too hard to keep track. (Okay, so that last one has absolutely nothing to do with what we're talking about here, but still.) Thanks to your cell phone—along with

Facebook, Twitter, Flickr, and whatever other accounts you have a username and password for—you can juggle your job, friendships, and relationships with nothing more than a double click. For the most part, the digital revolution has been a good thing, but all this e-everything has its drawbacks. Here we examine the positives and negatives of your online life.

SIGNED IN: A LOOK AT ALL ASPECTS OF YOUR SO-CALLED VIRTUAL LIFE

Maintaining the Status Update Quo: Online Social Networking

WHY WE LOVE IT: Like we mentioned earlier, Facebook and other social networking sites (except for MySpace, which has officially gone the way of the Discman) provide a great way to widen our social circles and reestablish old connections. Plus, these sites manage to simultaneously be the ultimate time-wasters (yay for *Mafia Wars*) and the ultimate time-savers. Hell, you don't even need to remember your friends' birthdays because Facebook does the remembering for you. Even better, you don't even need to write the obligatory "happy bday xoxo" text since you can just write it on her "wall." (That kind of enabling for our complete and utter laziness? Priceless.)

WHY WE HATE IT: If you refresh your Facebook page right now, chances are there will be at least ten new items in your news feed. That mean more photos of people's sleeping infants to look at, more new quizzes to take, and more status updates like, "I have a headache" to catch up on. What we're trying to say is that between uploading the photos from your recent trip to Turkey (it's so hot right now), reading twenty-five random things about the kid who sat next to you in eighth-grade social studies class, and comparing your life to that of your 632 "friends" (five of whom you actually speak to on a regular basis), social networking sites can feel a bit like a full-time job.

They also make us feel like we're one of those shut-ins who play life-simulation computer games instead of actually getting off the couch and interacting with real people. And the only thing worse than a social networking junkie who breaks out in a cold sweat if she hasn't updated her page in the past ten seconds is the person (usually it's a guy) who proudly refuses to join Facebook. You know, that same d-bag who held out on getting a cell phone until, like, 2002.

Twitter Me This: Microblogging

WHY WE LOVE IT: Isn't it obvious why we love Twitter? It enables us to read pearls of wisdom from the greatest philosophers of our time, such as Ashton Kutcher, Kanye West, and Courtney Love. We also love microblogging sites for a more practical reason: They keep us connected to our friends and family, as well as everyone and anyone else we might want to stalk, in a totally acceptable way. (Here's looking at you, Rachel Maddow.)

WHY WE HATE IT: Is it just us or does the whole "follow me on Twitter" thing kind of have the vibe of a middle school popularity contest? For example, if you follow seventy-two people but only four people follow you (one of them being your mother), does that make you a total loser? Also, it's bad enough that every person who uses Twitter chronicles what they're eating for lunch and watching on TV, but some also use it as a forum to announce some (in our opinion) very personal news. (@everyone-in-the-freaking-universe: water just broke and contractions are starting!) Plus, the 140-character limit makes everyone's tweets read like haikus that were written by a college student who just smoked some really bad (or perhaps really good) ganja.

(Im)Personal Communication: Email, Texting, and Instant Messaging

WHY WE LOVE IT: If you're thirty years old right now (plus or minus a few years), think back to college (try not to freak out when you realize how long ago it was) and a little place called the "computer cluster." For those of you who don't remember or went to better colleges than we did, the computer cluster was a windowless room where students would go to check their email once or twice a week using a university-administered password that was such a convoluted mix of letters, numbers, and symbols that you needed to write it on your hand in order to remember it. Back then, AOL Instant Messenger still had that creepy "what r u wearing?" vibe, and texting sounded like something people did after taking ecstasy. We've come a long freaking way since those days and are still slightly amazed at how ridiculously easy it is to communicate with your friends, significant others, family members, and coworkers.

WHY WE HATE IT: By now, these forms of techno-relating are so ingrained in our daily lives that it's hard to really hate on any of them. However, there is one thing that still gets our boy shorts in a bunch. Despite our years of experience with email, IM, and texting, communication breakdowns still run rampant. Since you can't hear a sender's tone of voice, see her facial expressions, or read her body language, it's all too easy to misinterpret the real meaning of the message. Plus, the computer acts as a shield that gives us the cojones to write things that we wouldn't normally say to someone's face. One of these days you just might lose your cool and respond to your boss's fourteenth email about expense reports with a few choice words ("fuck," "fucker," and "fucking" come to mind). Oops! To prevent this from happening, always remember that you shouldn't rage and write email. (And don't drink and email, either.)

There's an App for That: CrackBerries and iEverything

WHY WE LOVE IT: Once upon a time it was considered pretty damn techie to own a StarTAC cell phone and a ten-pound laptop. Then, we were introduced to the BlackBerry, an electronic marvel that let email arrive in the palm of our hands—a multitasker's dream come true. Fast-forward a few years and now everyone and her mother owns some version of a smartphone (no, seriously, Andrea's mother has one), essentially a mini mobile computer that you've loaded up with cool "apps" and sometimes even use to make phone calls. Thanks to these sleek handheld devices (which are considered more of a necessity than a gadget at this point), you can do everything from getting directions to a bar that's so cool it doesn't even have a sign to dividing up the bill (plus tip) for that intimate dinner with ten of your nearest and dearest friends. (Unfortunately, they haven't made an app yet that deals with the cheapskate of the bunch who insists that he didn't even touch the appetizers so he shouldn't have to pay as much as everyone else.) And let's not forget the biggest benefit of all: Never again will you be stuck in the waiting room at the gynecologist's office with nothing but a July/August 2007 issue of AARP's magazine for entertainment.

WHY WE HATE IT: We've become so addicted to our smartphones that we hear the tapping sound of thumbs furiously hitting tiny keys even in our sleep. That's because once you start using a BlackBerry or iPhone, it's nearly impossible to put the damn thing down. Ever. Not during dinner with your in-laws, an important work meeting, or even in the bathroom. (You know you do it, too.) And don't even get us started on people who interrupt a conversation to hold up their phone so Shazam can confirm that the song playing right now is indeed Shakira's latest guilty pleasure. However, none of these things compare to the ultimate drawback of CrackBerries and iEverything: the expectation that we are available to respond to email, phone calls, and text messages immediately upon receiving them. ("Local anesthesia means that you were still conscious, so tell me again why were you avoiding my phone calls?")

Upload Now: Online Photo Sites

WHY WE LOVE IT: Sharing photos used to be a labor-intensive undertaking. You either went for the free set of doubles at CVS, which your friends would inevitably fight over, or you got the negatives and threw them in a drawer, forgetting to get them developed. Today, with digital cameras and sites such as Flickr, SmugMug, and even Facebook, it takes seconds to upload shots of your birthday party or fabulous vacation to St. Wherever and share them with anyone you think might want to see them (and many people who probably don't). You can also see the pics your old college roommate posted of her two-year-old's dance recital. And the best part? All you have to do is write a nice comment ("omg she is so cute!!") and your friend duty is done. To sum it up (at the risk of sounding like a Kodak commercial), the latest photo-sharing technology lets us feel like we're a part of our friends' and families' lives, even if we can't be there in person.

WHY WE HATE IT: Every time we attend a social event, we have to contend with our own personal paparazzi completely unarmed, without the help of a stylist, makeup artist, and hair guru.

Look!—I Found Someone Who Will Sleep with Me on a Regular Basis: What Your Facebook Profile Photo Really Says about You

You don't have to bother with status updates or even filling out any of the personal info. The photo you've chosen tells everything we need to know about your life.

Your Profile Photo	What It Really Says About You
You and your significant other being all lovey-dovey and shmoopy-woopy☺	"We haven't had sex in eight months."

Your Profile Photo	What It Really Says About You
Your baby	"I've earned the right to use any profile photo I damn well please. Why, you might ask? One word: 'episiotomy.'"
A shot of you trying to look all hot, sexy, and come-hither (which is very fifteen-year-old-girl-on-MySpace, by the way)	"Someone, please give me the attention my father never gave me! Anyone? Please? Pretty please?"
You and your closest girl friends posing with cosmos during a girls' night out	"I'm so Carrie . . . or maybe I'm more Charlotte . . . or Miranda. . . . That's it. Maybe I'm a Miranda."
A photo of you in some exotic and faraway locale	"I like running away from my problems."
Your dog	"I'm not ready to go off birth control and start trying just *yet*."
No profile photo uploaded	"I don't have time for this shit." Or, better yet, "I want people to *think* I don't have time for this shit."
A picture of you all wasted	"I'm only fun when I'm drunk."
You and your cute gay guy friend	"Hopefully, someone will think this is my boyfriend."
You and someone else's baby	"Hopefully, someone will think I have sex."

Flashback: The Tao of Cher Horowitz

We think it's pretty clear. Unless, you were one of those people who peaked in high school, puberty sucked. On the bright side, there were plenty of movies from your adolescent years that didn't suck—or if they stunk it up, at least they fell into the so-bad-they're-good category. Below, we detail some of our favorite teen-angsty films. Sure, they're great to watch on a Sunday morning as you recover from a hangover, but they also provide many valuable lessons that still apply to your life today.

THE FLICK: *Clueless*

A BRIEF REFRESHER: As *if* you don't remember every freaking line of this movie. Loosely based on Jane Austen's *Emma*, *Clueless* chronicles the life of rich, popular teen with a heart of twenty-four-karat gold Cher Horowitz (played by Alicia Silverstone, fresh off her roles as a hot underage crazy chick in *The Crush* and a hot underage crazy chick in some classic Aerosmith videos). Even though Cher has everything—from a glam house in Beverly Hills (complete with a fully computerized closet) to a fab posse that paved the way for the Plastics (let's hear it for Dionne)—she longs for something more. When her crunchy-granola ex-stepbrother accuses her of being superficial and selfish (Cher: "I have direction!" Josh: "Yeah, to the mall."), Cher vows to prove him wrong and heads down a frilly pink path of self-discovery—while wearing a plaid skirt and thigh-high stockings, natch. Along the way, she rolls with the homies, recalibrates her gaydar, discovers a flair for philanthropy, and, of course, finds true love.

WHAT YOU CAN LEARN FROM THIS MOVIE TODAY: Okay, so we know that this is going to sound a little creepy, but if your ex-stepbrother is as half as cute as Paul Rudd, we say go for it. Oh, and don't forget Cher's surprisingly practical advice about drug use ("It is one thing to spark up a doobie and get laced at parties, but it is quite another to be fried all day"), which still holds true when you're older. You can also take another cue from our vivacious Valley girl, who organizes a charity drive at the end of the movie. If you don't do so already, try volunteering your time for a worthy cause. Helping others will make you feel good, and it will put the problems and tumultuousness that you're experiencing during the redo-berty years into perspective.

THE FLICK: Any Teen Movie John Hughes Ever Made (Note: We lumped these all together because they could fill up an entire book.)

A BRIEF REFRESHER: When auteur extraordinaire John Hughes passed away, we felt like part of our youth did, too. Although his charming tales of adolescent angst (*The Breakfast Club, Pretty in Pink, Some Kind of Wonderful, Sixteen Candles,* and *Ferris Bueller's Day Off*) predated our own adolescent years, they will be forever fresh and cool, even to generations who didn't wear neon and leggings the first time around. Class struggles, alienation, funky fashions, family issues, Molly Ringwald, first loves, and killer soundtracks—John had something in there for everyone, but his movies really championed the geeks, dweebs, spazzes, and other outsiders who felt like they would eat alone in the cafeteria forever.

WHAT YOU CAN LEARN FROM THESE MOVIES TODAY: A few lessons learned for John Hughes's films: (1) Money can't buy you love.

(2) Dance to the beat of your own drummer and everything else will be all right. (3) And the geeks shall inherit the earth. And, most important of all, (4) Never *ever* trust a guy who pops his collar. Oh, you may think we're joking, but we're not, dear reader. Oh, we're not. In fact, we'll go so far as to say that you should be wary of anyone who fully embraces trends that were once popular in the eighties but have reared their Flock of Seagulls–coiffed heads again at Urban Outfitters.

THE FLICK: *Dazed and Confused*

A BRIEF REFRESHER: Oh, how we longed to have come of age during the 1970s! Actually, we should rephrase that. Oh, how we longed to come of age during the 1970s as depicted in *Dazed and Confused*! It's the last day of classes at Lee High School in Texas, and teenage rites of passage take center stage. Following tradition, soon-to-be seniors initiate members of the incoming freshman class, garnering twisted pleasure from making their lives miserable. The boys get beat in the ass with a wooden paddle and the girls are subjected to the type of humiliation usually reserved for sorority pledges. But it's all in good fun—we swear! Set to a killer soundtrack, this film also features disenfranchised youth doing what they do best: getting stoned, drinking beer in the woods, and driving around town looking for a place to get stoned and drink beer. As an added bonus, the cast includes certified girl crush Parker Posey, Jason London (our favorite of the twins) as the football player who just wants to cut loose without the Man (a.k.a. his coach) breathing down his neck, and Matthew McConaughey, in his best role ever, playing that sleazy guy of indeterminate age who left high school years ago but still hangs around at all the parties, hoping to get lucky with a girl who is too young to know any better. ("That's what I love about these high school girls, man. I get older, they stay the same age.")

WHAT YOU CAN LEARN FROM THIS MOVIE TODAY: Stick up for what you believe in. Just like Pink (Jason London) refused to sign a pledge promising not to spend the summer getting totally blazed, you should totally stand up to those Nazis in HR and tell them just where they can shove that paltry cost-of-living raise. Yeah! Rage against the machine! Actually, this movie also had a couple of other great life lessons, summed up in the following memorable quotes. From Cynthia (the adorably geeky one with the red 'fro): "If we're all gonna die anyway, shouldn't we be enjoying ourselves now?" And, from our favorite London brother: "All I'm saying is that if I ever start referring to these as the best years of my life—remind me to kill myself." In other words, have fun and realize that your best years are the ones in front of you. (Case in point: Have you hung out with your mother and her friends lately? You can barely keep up with them!) Also, even though you lead the busy life of a responsible adult, make sure to step off of the treadmill every once in a while and enjoy an evening of just hanging out with your friends with no illusions, no pretensions, and no pressure.

THE FLICK: *Can't Hardly Wait*

A BRIEF REFRESHER: Sticking to the tried-and-true teen movie formula, *Can't Hardly Wait* takes place at a graduation party. The plot follows five very different students, each with a special plan for making it the best night ever—because we all know that nothing will ever be as fun as high school!! Cue Sarah McLachlan's "I Will Remember You" or Green Day's "Good Riddance (Time of Your Life)." Popular girl Amanda (Jennifer Love Hewitt) finds her world turned upside down when her dumb jock boyfriend, Mike (Peter Facinelli), dumps her to free him up for an inevitable sexual awakening in college, where he will realize that he prefers big, burly tight ends both on and off the field. (See the story of Scott Sadowsky on page 102.) Preston (Ethan

Embry) pines for Amanda's jugs—we mean, her *mind*—so he pens a love letter in the hopes that he'll be able to cop a feel—we mean, let her know how he *feels*. Denise (Lauren Ambrose) hates everything, but she goes on to star in *Six Feet Under*, one of the best television shows ever, so it's all good. And, finally, Kenny (Seth Green), a red-headed wannabe rapper just wants some poon, y'all, and by wanting some poon (yes, we hate that word, too, but as you'll later find out when you read about our love-hate relationship with *nesting*, we can't help but use it sometimes), we mean that he's actually an innocent, fragile virgin who just wants to be loved. In his no-no spot. By the end of this movie—surprise, surprise—all of the characters get what they want, but there are some surprises along the way that we won't ruin because we're selfless like that.

WHAT YOU CAN LEARN FROM THIS MOVIE TODAY: There's nothing like an amazing karaoke performance to improve your social standing. Just ask William Lichter, the geeky kid who belted out "Paradise City" at the infamous graduation night party. According to the movie's epilogue, he becomes one of the most popular students at Harvard and goes on to form his own computer company that makes him millions. And, oh yeah—he's dating a supermodel.

THE FLICK: *She's All That*

A BRIEF REFRESHER: High school heartthrob Zack makes a bet with his friends that he can transform Laney (Rachael Leigh Cook) into the prom queen. He really has his work cut out for him, though, because—get this—Laney wears glasses (yuck!), wants to be an artist (gross!), and pulls her hair back into a ponytail (excuse us while we go and barf somewhere!). After a radical makeover, which includes removing her glasses, Laney is transformed into a bona fide fox whom Zack wants to bone—sorry, we mean, love and cherish forever. This was a PG-13-rated movie, after all. Drama ensues when

Laney discovers that she was part of a bet, but everything works out in the end, and, mostly important, Zack discovers that he has a very viable skill: kicking a hackey sack while reciting corny faux-artsy monologues ("Never . . . let . . . it . . . drop!").

WHAT YOU CAN LEARN FROM THIS MOVIE TODAY: Actually, don't listen to what this movie told you. Guys do in fact make passes at girls who wear glasses. Find someone who will like you for you—glasses, overalls, and ponytail (oh, the horror!)—the whole package.

THE FLICK: *10 Things I Hate About You*
A BRIEF REFRESHER: Much like *She's All That*, this movie involves a guy, a girl on the fringes of society, and an exchange of money. (Actually, when we put it that way, this sounds a lot like HBO's creepy yet fascinating classic late-night doc *Hookers at the Point*.) In *10 Things I Hate About You*, thanks to her bordering-on-Joe-Simpson-creepy father, bubbly high school golden girl Bianca (Larisa Oleynik) isn't allowed to date until her angry, riot grrrl sister Kat (Julia Stiles) does. In a stroke of genius, one of Bianca's admirers, Cameron (cutie Joseph Gordon-Levitt), masterminds a plan to get the girl of his dreams. He convinces a slimy popular guy to pay mysterious bad boy Patrick (Heath Ledger) to take Kat out and show her a good time, which in turn would free Bianca from her dad's no-dating rule and drive her right into Cameron's arms. All of this is very complicated (we're too lazy to detail it in a flow chart), so if you're not following, don't worry. All you need to know is that there's one scene where Julia Stiles's character gets plastered and does a sexy version of "The Elaine" on top of a kitchen table at a house party that makes us wonder how she ever got cast in *Save the Last Dance*.

WHAT YOU CAN LEARN FROM THIS MOVIE TODAY: Before you go out on a blind date, make sure that there isn't a cash reward in it for the guy. If that's the case, you two will inevitably fall in love. Of course, once you fall in love, the bet will somehow be revealed, breaking your heart, and it will be hard for the guy to win you back without a prom to make everything better.

Sounding Off

As we've been saying all along, there is no "right" way to live your life as a responsible, functional adult, so long as, you know, you're responsible and functional. Of course, there are a few rules of thumb. For example, if you fight with friends via Twitter or you've recently pulled out a bitch's weave because she gave you a dirty look at the club (she was just jealous), then you probably still have a bit of growing up left to do.

Anyway, we asked some random real adult women who range in age from 26 to 32.5 (we love the ".5") about their lives, hopes, and dreams during the redo-berty years. You'll read their answers, which range from poignant to hilarious, throughout the book. Let's start on a high note with the upside of the redo-berty years. We asked them the following: **What's the best part about being in your late twenties/early thirties?**

"Still being able to blame my bullshit choices on my relative youth. Having hope for the future. Having room to grow."—*Sara, 28*

"Doing crazy things, dating crazy people, wearing crazy outfits, and *not* worrying about what other people think."—*Carla, 27*

"Having enough money to actually do things."—*Brooke, 29*

"I'm more confident about my comfort zone than I was in my early twenties. These days, I'm fine with my likes, dislikes, hobbies, and really don't care at all about where I fit in on the mainstream scale."—*Julie, 30*

"I know who my friends are more than ever. At this point, it's like survival of the fittest—the frenemies have fallen by the wayside by now, whereas in your early twenties and during your college years, there was a sense of obligation to stay friends with certain people."—*Jackie, 29*

"The best thing about being in my early thirties is knowing not only who I am but being comfortable with it as well. I've become a fun, fulfilled, confident person in the last five years—more than I ever thought I'd be, had I been asked in my early twenties. I've come to learn it's okay to say no, it's okay to make your own rules, and it's okay to agree to disagree and still be friends with someone."—*Lis, 32*

"For me the best part was definitely my relationship. I found someone that I am truly at ease with and would be content if it were just the two of us stuck on an island together. I also feel like I have developed better relationships with friends, realized it truly is quality over quantity."—*Melissa, 30*

"Being married with one child and another on the way, but still feeling like a young, hip mom."—*Lori, 30*

"You can change jobs, careers, and boyfriends without completely ripping your life apart. Also, I like that you can shop at Forever 21 until you are about thirty-five. That place is cheap!"—*Jen, 26*

"Knowing who I am. Or at least knowing who I am more than I did when I was in college. Going to grad school gave me the opportunity to enter into dialogues with people I would never had been friends with as an undergraduate. I admitted to myself that I was indeed gay, something that my super-Catholic undergraduate mind had forced into submission. By coming out to myself, and later others, I was able to find a comfort in my own skin that I had been faking since the ninth grade."—*Danielle, 26*

"The confidence that comes along with it. I feel like I finally know who I am and what I can do. I am also so much more self-aware and once you are self-aware you can work on your deficits." —*Laura, 32.5*

Three

Coping Mechanisms:
What Type of Adult Are You?

Rob Fleming: Fuck. I hate all this stuff. How old do you have to get before it stops?"

—from *High Fidelity*

DURING YOUR puberty years, you dealt with change by slipping into and out of different personas like they were shoes, going from girly girl to jockess to goth to hippie chick before finally ending up with the real you, who is most likely a combination of all of those things. Sure, you're older now and no longer grapple with uncertainty and upheaval by dyeing your hair black, covering your face with white foundation, and worshipping at the altar of the Cure. Still, the redoberty years can cause some degree of identity struggle, a response to pressures and expectations of adulthood. Read on to see where your reactions (or overreactions) fit in and what type of adult you are. (And before we continue, we know that there are as many types of adults as there are Tyler Perry movies, but you'll probably recognize yourself in one of the following archetypes.)

SENIORITIS: THE PREMATURE GRANNY

WHAT'S YOUR STORY? The last time you skimmed through a magazine while waiting in line at the grocery store, you passed over "Seven

Steamy Secrets of Sexier Sex" and went right to "Eight Simple Ways to Improve You Memory." You've started leaving concerts before the encore in order to "beat the traffic," and you rarely wear high heels (they aggravate your bunion) or stay up later than 11:30 p.m. (OK, so you made it to 11:50 on New Year's Eve, only barely missing the ball drop—on TV.) Plus, you can't understand why anyone would want to take a cardio striptease class, and is it cold in here or is it just you?

If age is indeed a mental state, then your brain has retired early and migrated south to the Republic of AARP (a.k.a. Florida) to hang out with the Centrum Silver club. That's right, Nana: You're a woman in her prime who's got a case of Senioritis. You're the Premature Granny.

WHAT'S REALLY GOING ON: According to an unscientific poll, Senioritis affects one in five women in their late twenties and early thirties. It's most common in those who spent their teens and young adult years partying harder than a tragic starlet and feel like they need to overcompensate by becoming more chaste than a Disney Channel star pretends to be.

Another explanation might be that you're unnecessarily terrified of becoming some sort of sad cougar in the bar who's trying to prove that she's "still got it" in a boob shirt, miniskirt, and hoochie heels. (Hey, we say if you got it, flaunt it.) So, instead of growing up and hanging out at places that don't specialize in Jell-O shots and wet T-shirt contests, you prematurely choose not to go out at all. Unless of course Josh "Voice of an Angel" Groban is in town.

THE PREMATURE GRANNY'S FAVORITE SAYINGS

At first your friends found your geriatric quips humorous, but now you're giving them flashbacks to high school when they volunteered at a local nursing home because it looked good on their college applications.

1. "Can you turn down the AC?"
2. "Make mine a decaf."
3. "It's just like in that episode of *Matlock* . . ."
4. "I have a bad back/trick knee/spastic colon."
5. "Social Security is in the shitter."
6. "I'm trying to eat more fiber."
7. "Thong underwear just seems unhygienic."
8. "I'd never let my daughter leave the house in that."
9. "Why is the music so loud in here?"
10. "I'd rather get a good night's sleep."
11. "I'm such an old lady."

HOW TO GET A LIFE: There isn't an official rulebook that dictates how a grown-up should behave; however, there's something wrong with a woman in the prime of her life who drinks prune juice and lets out an involuntary grunt whenever she gets up from the couch. Hit your inner rewind button and get your ass to the gym (just ditch that ridiculous-looking pedometer) lest you regret not using it when you *really* lose it several decades from now.

FOREVER 21: THE I-WON'T-GROW-UP ADULT

WHAT'S YOUR STORY? As you approach and pass the big 3-0, many of your friends are already wrapped up in "adult life," wrestling with mortgages, marriages, and babies. Your priorities, on the other hand, remain simple and clear: liquor before beer. That's because you're the Forever 21, the post-quarterlifer who won't grow up. To quote the 1985 hit song by thespian-cum-troubadour Eddie Murphy, you want to "party all the time, party all the time, party all the ti-ime." And party you do. Last Friday, after winning first place in a beer pong tournament, you commemorated your victory by getting into a cat-fight outside of the bar. Then, after the police left without filing an incident report, you went to a club in a converted warehouse space to watch a tragically hip Swedish deejay spin for a tragically hip crowd. It was there that you met Sebastian, a really cute guy who took you to an after-hours party . . . in his dorm room.

There's nothing wrong with cutting loose after a long day, but when pesky little things like your job or your liver start to get in the way of your busy social calendar (which consists of evenings spent knocking back Jägermeister shots at the bar, yelling "Wooo!" until you lose your voice, and shaking your junk on the dance floor), it might be time to extinguish that Marlboro Light and leave the freshman-year lifestyle where it belongs: in college. And before you say something original like "Age is only a number" or "You're only as old as you feel," consider this: How do you actually feel when you wake up at 1 p.m. on a Sunday "morning"? Enjoying yourself and embracing life doesn't need to involve embracing the toilet bowl at the end of the night. You don't always have to be the last one to leave the party, Tara Reid. And while we're at it, why the hell are you wearing pigtails?

YOU MIGHT BE FOREVER 21 IF . . .
1. You identify with the "characters" on *The Real World*.
2. You still own Yaffa blocks.
3. You hung up pictures from spring break in your cube.
4. You wear flip-flops with formal wear, Uggs with denim miniskirts, and sweatpants with something written across the ass.
5. The bouncers at the bars in your town know you by name.
6. All of your friends use your old driver's license to get in everywhere.
7. Sushi = SAKE BOMBS!
8. Most nights, you pass out rather than fall asleep.

9. Your credit card bill is sent directly to your parents' house.
10. For you, the food pyramid consists of Pizza Rolls, Hot Pockets, and Papa John's.
11. You think that what college you went to is actually important.
12. You think that *you* are actually important.

WHAT'S REALLY GOING ON: You don't have to be Dr. Phil or even a real psychologist to figure out why you're acting like a teenage celebrity who just had her first Red Bull and vodka. It's hard to accept that you're not the youngest woman in the room anymore, but throwing your life in reverse won't help.

HOW TO GET A LIFE: Get pregnant and then torture your child with a name like Kombucha Tea or iPod! We hear that's the best way to grow up overnight. We kid, we kid. For starters, stop viewing getting older as an affliction for which the only cure is a round (or five) of Jolly Rancher martinis at happy hour with your interns from work. It's also important to recognize that you look sort of ridiculous dressing and acting like an overgrown teenager. You'll feel more secure about your situation if you own it. So, adopt a dog, sign up for an evening class, or join a book club (which is just a front for gossiping over several bottles of wine, anyway).

SOY: THE SUDDEN-ONSET YUPPIE

WHAT'S YOUR STORY? Ah, the follies of youth. It seems like only yesterday that your wine knowledge was limited to Franzia and Carlo Rossi and your furniture consisted of a futon and a butterfly chair. Then, seemingly overnight, a fairy (OK, WASPy) godmother tapped you with her wand, and—poof!—not since Becky Gerber left for summer camp in seventh grade wearing a training bra and came back to school in September sporting a rack that a million inappropriate gym teachers would risk seven to ten years for has there been such a magical transformation.

Yes, you, the girl who used to drink white zinfandel out of a box and decorate with shabby-unchic dorm decor, morphed into a woman who actually cares about the vintage of her Pinot, the thread count of her sheets, and a bunch of other proper "adult" things that your twenty-year-old self would've scoffed at. (Think: dinner parties, Whole Foods, Starbucks compilation CDs, charity fund-raiser boards, original woodwork, and any of that other stuff white people like.)

Now, everyone has different tastes, so if boat shoes float your boat or you're a sucker for seersucker, who are we to judge? Plus, there's nothing wrong with wanting to upgrade to nicer stuff as you get older. (After all, a woman can't live on ramen alone.) You just need to ask yourself this question: Do I really like architecture, artisanal cheeses, and art exhibits, or do I *think* I have to like them because I'm a big girl now, which means that I have to fulfill other people's big expectations of how a successful adult should be? If you follow the gospel according to the *New York Times* Style section and Williams-Sonoma, we've got a diagnosis for your condition: You're a Sudden-Onset Yuppie, or SOY, for short. (And, for the record, the yuppies of today are a bit crunchier than their Alex P. Keatonish 1980s counterparts, who favored a conservative fiscal policy, bragged about their state-of-the-art VCRs, and snorted coke while rocking out to the latest Huey Lewis and the News cassette tape.

The SOY: Then and Now

Can you believe there was a time when you used regular table salt instead of *fleur de sel*? Well, you should because it was last week. Here, a look at how your taste has evolved in warp speed.

Yesterday	Today
Sending a text message	Sending a handwritten note on engraved monogrammed stationery
Going dancing at the club with your gays	Going to a knitting class with your lesbian neighbors
Emma for a girl and Max for a boy	Matilda for a girl and Stellan for a boy
Rice	Quinoa
Playing beer pong	Playing Scrabble
Dating a guy for his looks	Dating a guy for his credit rating
Taking a yoga class	Taking a yoga class . . . with your dog
Bitching about the line at the door	Bitching about the reservations policy
Reading celebrity tabloids	Reading home decorating magazines
Crashing	Nesting
Smoking green	Being green
Chugging beer	Nursing your gluten allergy
ADHD	IBS

WHAT'S REALLY GOING ON: For a guy, the SOY phenomenon often happens when he finally meets a girl he likes and she introduces him to a wonder known as a "duvet cover." On the other hand, those of us with a vagina find our way to SOYdom via different avenues. Perhaps you've gone soft in your older age, and those commercials about global warming with the momma and baby polar bears stranded on a lone piece of ice have melted your cold heart, and now you're committed to ensuring that your future children will live in a world with polar bears . . . and wear T-shirts made out of bamboo . . . and go to private kindergartens that cost more than private colleges. Or perhaps you're finally making enough money to upgrade from the Martha Stewart Collection. (Authors' note: We happen to think that the M-Dawg makes some fine bedding. So there!)

Like we said before, there's nothing wrong with having an herb garden or a wine fridge, but you should be nesting because you *want* to nest, not because *The Nest* told you to. (By the way, the word "nesting" makes us sick. More about that in Chapter 10.) Part of becoming a real adult is growing up on your terms rather than losing yourself as you try to live up to someone else's expectations and stepping into a life that resembles *American Psycho*, minus the dead hookers. And, don't forget that maturity and a sense of responsibility make you a grown-up, not monogrammed towels and a sense of entitlement. However, those towels are, like, totally cute.

SOY WARNING SIGNS

Here are some red flags that you might be taking your newfound interest in upwardly mobile adulthood a little too seriously.

1. You're willing to pay $2,500 for a mutt.
2. You refer to your husband as your "DH" (or your significant other as your "SO") on Facebook.
3. You're willing to stand in line to buy an iPod/iPhone/iWhatever.
4. You think it's cute when toddlers eat sushi.
5. You use "summer" as a verb.
6. You have the type of strong opinion on breast-feeding that is

usually reserved for more important stuff like wars. (You know, because no one in the history of humanity has every breast-fed.)

7. You're saving up for an SUV . . . a Volvo SUV.
8. You served salted caramel gelato for dessert at your last dinner party.
9. You registered for a $600 Alessi espresso maker and fully expect someone to buy it for you.
10. You became a fan of *All Things Considered* on Facebook.
11. You're starting a blog—about cupcakes.

HOW TO GET A LIFE: There's nothing wrong with acquiring a taste for the finer things in life, but keep in mind that no one is going to revoke your official adult membership card if you drink beer out of the can, eat a bowl of Kraft Macaroni & Cheese, or watch a big-budget action flick. If you're killing yourself to make your life look J.Crew-catalog perfect, maybe it's time to put down the glue gun and die cutter and figure out what's really bothering you. (Not to play doctor, but perhaps it has something to do with your awful childhood?)

THE EARLY-DECISION ADULT:
MARRIED WITH A MORTGAGE AND A MINIVAN

WHAT'S YOUR STORY? Maybe it was because you always preferred Samantha to Charlotte (like our sick fascination with the word "puberty"—and, as you'll read later on in this book, our love-hate affair with "nesting"—we can't help making a few *Sex and the City* references). Or perhaps it was the incident involving you, half a tray of Jell-O shots, and Dave Giordano at the Delta Sig "G.I. Joes and Army Hoes" party. Whatever the reason, no one (especially Dave Giordano) would've predicted that the same girl who gave away a goldfish because it was too much responsibility would have all of life's big to-do's—marriage, children, mortgage—checked off by her thirtieth birthday. But here you are: a real, live grown-up.

While the rest of your friends are cruising Match.com, refilling their birth control prescriptions, and checking out a new band at the hipster bar downtown, you're celebrating your fifth wedding anniversary, tracking your ovulation via an iPhone app, and taking your two-year-old to a Mini Maestros music class. That's why the Early-Decision Adult usually seeks out "mommy friends," a sorority of diaper bag–toting, breast milk–pumping, "take that out of your mouth" women who understand why you absolutely *had* to get a bikini wax before giving birth and truly give a shit that your toddler can count to twenty (he's a genius, we know). We're not saying that if you're the first one of your friends to get married and have children, your former life will immediately evaporate into thin air, but you have to admit that it's a little weird to have more in common with the girls on MTV's *Teen Mom* than with the ones you've known for almost two decades.

WHAT'S REALLY GOING ON: OK, so maybe "Early-Decision Adult" is a bit of a misnomer, considering that the average age of first marriage for women in the United States is around twenty-six years of age and the average age of a mother when she has her first child is twenty-five. You're a normal adult, just not when it comes to your group of friends. But don't sweat it. You could teach us a few things, big girl!

TEN SIGNS YOU NEED TO GET OUT MORE

We know that you can't exactly leave your kid at home every night of the week, but there's a reason why God created baby-sitters. (For the record, we can't believe that they get, like, twenty bucks an hour.) Here are some signs that you need to take some rare, yet much-needed, me-time.

1. The last time you went to a bar, you ordered a cosmopolitan.
2. You've never seen an episode of *Mad Men*, but you own *The Best of Elmo's World DVD Collection.*
3. Your most recent Facebook status update contained the phrase "pee-pee in the potty."
4. You wear your husband's sweatpants . . . in public.
5. You learned Spanish from watching *Dora the Explorer.*
6. You've had the song "Baby Beluga" stuck in your head for two years.
7. The last pair of jeans you bought had an elastic "bump band."
8. You schedule sex.
9. You spell out curse words even when there aren't any children around.
10. One of your mommy friends offered you a joint at a playdate. (Being a responsible parent, you declined, of course.)

HOW TO GET A LIFE: We feel kind of weird giving you a reality check considering you're the one who is a real, functioning adult. So, uh, yeah, would it be cool if we called you in a few years to ask you about organic diapers? Here is some advice that you can use: Just because you have your own family now doesn't mean that you should do whatever your virtual friends on mommy message boards tell you to do. You're your own person, and you're doing just fine without morphing into a mommybot.

Quiz: Do You Act Your Age?

Someone typically uses the phrase "Age is only a number" when she's trying to make herself feel better about an upcoming birthday or justify sleeping with Hugh Hefner. Now, we're not suggesting that there's only one way to behave during your redo-berty years, but there are certain expectations of adulthood, like you shouldn't *want* to live with your parents. Even if they have a guesthouse. Take this quiz to find out how close the number on your driver's license is to your *real* age.

Answer the following questions:

1. Your drink of choice:
a. A nice, robust red
b. JÄGERBOMBS!
c. Mylanta

2. True or false: Is it loud in here, or is it just us?
a. WHAT?! I CAN'T HEAR YOU!
b. False

3. What are your plans this Friday night?
a. Checking out that new tapas place with your friends
b. JÄGERBOMBS!
c. Donning your Snuggie, curling up on the couch, and watching reruns of *To Catch a Predator*

4. Complete the following analogy. Tube tops are to bars as ___:
a. Ping-Pong balls are to beer.
b. Sweaters are to small dogs.
c. Leashes are to children.

5. True or false: JÄGERBOMBS!
a. True
b. False
c. Wooooooooooooo!

6. Complete the following analogy. Shuttlecock is to badminton as ___ is to shuffleboard.
a. Hehe . . . you said "cock."
b. A disc
c. Tube tops are to bars

7. Fun with acronyms: What does DH stand for?
a. Don Henley
b. Dry Humping
c. Dear Husband

8. True or False: *Everybody Loves Raymond*
a. True
b. False

9. What are you sitting on right now? (You can skip over this question if it's the toilet.)
a. My ass
b. My Jennifer Convertibles Microfiber Dual Recliner with my DH
c. My couch, which is covered with protective plastic and within arm's reach of a bowl of Werther's Originals

10. Okay, no, let's try a little experiment. Stand up from where you are sitting. What just happened?
 a. I made a grunting sound.
 b. I made a grunting sound and my knees cracked.
 c. I made a grunting sound because I accidentally knocked over my bong and it cracked.

11. What was your last tweet?
 a. @JAGERBOMBS!
 b. @BedBathNBeyond with DH and we remembered the coupons this time. YAY!
 c. My last what? I don't think that's any of your business!

12. Your trusted news source:
 a. *E! News*
 b. NPR
 c. CNN.com

13. Who is your favorite Kate?
 a. Moss
 b. Gosselin
 c. Winslet

14. Who is your favorite Joe?
 a. G.I. Joe
 b. Jonas
 c. Biden

Answer Key (add up the total number of points for your answers):
 1. a: 2; b: 1; c: 3
 2. a: 2; b: 1

3. a: 2; b: 1; c: 3
4. a: 1; b: 2; c: 3
5. a: 2; b: 3; c: 1
6. a: 1; b: 3; c: 2
7. a: 3; b: 1; c: 2
8. a: 2; b: 1
9. a: 1; b: 2; c: 3
10. a: 2; b: 3; c: 1
11. a: 1; b: 2; c: 3
12. a: 1; b: 3; c: 2
13. a: 1; b: 3; c: 2
14. a: 1; b: 2; c: 3

If you scored:

14-20: You're underage.

OMG! You're, like, totally Benjamin Button! We know that being an adult can really suck at times (hence, why we wrote this book), but the answer isn't at the bottom of a shot glass. It's at the bottom of a wineglass.

21-30: You're age-appropriate.

Congratulations! As far as this quiz goes, you're the closest thing to a "normal" adult. Go ahead and celebrate. For all of your good work, we'll allow you a drunken sorority girl "Woooo!" (But just this once.)

31-40: You're overage.

Oh sorry, Nana, did we wake you up from your nap? It's one thing to be mature for your age but quite another to relate more to the ladies on *The Golden Girls* than *Gossip Girl*. Actually, we take that back because Dorothy, Blanche, Rose, and Sophia have a swingin' social life. So act more like them. You and the DH (or SO) can unspoon every once in a while and leave the nest.

Part II

Mature Content: All Aspects of Your So-Called Life

Think of this part of the book as *You: The Owner's Manual,* minus the talk about icky things like your GI tract and your circulatory system. In the following pages, we present a user's guide to all aspects of you during the redo-berty years, from your love life (or lack of one) to your career (or lack of one). Enjoy!

Four

———

At Least You're Not an Assistant Anymore: Your Career Aspirations, or What if Your Parachute Is Plaid?

One of the symptoms of an approaching nervous breakdown is the belief that one's work is terribly important.

—Bertrand Russell*

WORKING FOR THE WEEKEND

Think back to a time when you were young, innocent, and firmly believed that if you placed an extracted tooth beneath your pillow when you went to sleep at night, a fairy would flit into your bedroom and leave cold, hard cash behind in exchange for an incisor, canine, or molar. No, we're not talking about that one night in Prague during your backpacking jaunt across Europe post-sophomore year, when you drank too much absinthe at a discotheque and experienced crazy hallucinations. Think back to life as a kid, even before the hormones from puberty set in, when having an imaginary friend was a sign of creativity rather than mental illness and the only thing you would ever get high on was the Technicolor sugar from Pixy Stix. What did you want to be when you grew up? A ballerina? (Tutus are killer.) A mermaid? (Come to think of it, Ariel did have enviable hair.) A

———

* No relation to Keri Russell

supermarket checkout girl? (Scanning + pressing buttons = pure magic.) An astronaut? A police officer? A substitute teacher? A veterinarian? An actress?

Whatever you dreamed of becoming, chances are that it didn't include planting your rump on an office chair for countless hours each day and spewing out nonsense about "touching base" and "interfacing," your sole creative outlet coming at lunch when you get to choose the toppings for your Subway six-inch turkey sandwich. We're also absolutely positive that you didn't dream of growing up to become an adult who gave her best softball-playing years to one company, only to be called into an impromptu meeting one fateful afternoon and unceremoniously downsized, let go, and tossed aside like a starter wife. (Boy, oh boy, did you have to summon the self-restraint of a thousand nuns to keep your fist from "touching base" with the face of Denise, your she-douche of an HR director, as she insincerely wished you the best of luck in your future endeavors.)

Unless you're one of the lucky few who love going to work every morning (and if you are, we'd like to have what you're having/smoking), you've probably experienced job-related anxiety to some degree, ranging from mild (battling occasional bouts of burnout) to major (struggling to make it through the day without shoving a company-branded pen through your eyeball). In a society where we work hard (according to some studies, Americans are the most productive employees in the world), play hardly at all (we're taking fewer vacation days than ever before, thanks to sickly state of the economy), and derive much of our identity from what we do to pay the bills (too much, in our opinion), it's not surprising that you feel a wee bit angst-ridden about your professional life.

You've reached an age when you're young enough that you still might be unsettled career-wise, but old enough to start worrying that maybe you shouldn't be. This confusing time is when redo-berty starts creeping in. You look around at your peers, compare their *metaphorical* racks to your, um, *allegorical* flat chest (yeah, we're just throwing around the AP English terms), and furiously scrawl in your little pink journal at night: *Dear Diary: It's just NOT fair! Katie got promoted to regional manager and Jenny has an expense account and I'm going to die alone as a temp worker, and no boy is ever going kiss me!*

These old insecurities—fearing that you'll be left in the dust as your peer groups forges ahead, worrying that you aren't normal, and dreading that you're somehow not living up to others' expectations—are as classic as a little black dress.

The New Coming of Age Moments: Career Edition

Remember when you thought that the coolest part of being an adult was the fact that you never had to do homework again? Little did you know that you'd be trading in book reports and dioramas for PowerPoint presentations and memos. Here are the professional equivalents to your academic triumphs and tragedies.

Puberty	Redo-berty
Trying out for the cheerleading squad and getting cut during the first round	Interviewing for a job and never hearing back from HR
Catching a glimpse of your mousy lab partner's boobies while changing in the locker room and realizing that she's way more stacked than you are	Catching a glimpse of your incompetent coworker's pay stub while making photocopies and realizing that she makes way more than you do
Stumbling across Mr. Miller's "secret" video stash (with titles	Stumbling across your married boss's Match.com profile . . . in the
(continued)	(continued)

Puberty	Redo-berty
like *Big Trouble in Little Vagina* and *Moulin Splooge*) while baby-sitting his kids	men-seeking-men section (screen name: MrsZacEfron).
Tossing your cookies all over your Dyeables at the Homecoming dance	Tossing your cookies all over your Aerosoles at the holiday office party
Winning your school's student council election	Winning your office's March Madness pool
Getting sent home from school for wearing a crop top	Getting a warning from HR for wearing flip-flops (even though they were totally cute Havianas)
Sporting the "Rachel" in your yearbook photo	Sporting the "Suri Cruise" in your security ID photo
Pimping your notebooks with Lisa Frank stickers	Pimping your internal memos with neon-colored Post-it notes
Dealing with Queen Bees, Mean Girls, and Bullies who think they rule the school	Dealing with Queen Bees, Mean Girls, and Bullies who think they rule the cubicles (some things never change)

We're here to tell you, our savvy soul-searchers, that it's going to be all right. Don't believe us? Then perhaps you'll listen to the Department of Labor, which reports that the average person goes through eight jobs before reaching thirty-two years of age. The moral of the story is this: We all find our own way, and just because your best friend has a corner office while you're stuck in a job you hate doesn't make you an inadequate person who will never make it to first base with a boy. Plus, let's have a little reality check. In an economy that's less stable than a stripper who's competing for the affections of an eighties rock star with a weave, you need to realize that you're actually in good company. No one—neither the newbies nor the twenty-five-year veterans of the industry—has job security these days. And before we ask you if you want a little cheese with that *whine*, be thankful if you can move from job to job and only have yourself rather than a family to worry about supporting.

Now, let's take a look at where you might be in the world of 9 to 5 (which is really more like 9 to 8 on a good day, you workaholic, you).

Some Possible Scenarios: Where You're at with Your Professional Life

STUCK IN CRUISE CONTROL: You've been at your job for a few years, and the pay is decent, the people are nice, and—assuming that your newlywed manager's ovulation predictor is correct—you should be getting her job in nine months. Yet you feel increasingly bored/disillusioned/trapped/depressed and are thinking about quitting your job to go back to school/open up a bakery/start an escort service. So what's holding you back from making a change? Maybe it's because of the constant reminders about how lucky you are to have a job right now. Or maybe you're clueless as to what you want to do with your life and that uncertainty has left you paralyzed. Or it could come down a practical (and extremely legitimate) reason: fear of disrupting your regular paycheck. The good news is that job experts say you don't have to actually quit your job to get out of your rut. You could volunteer to work on a project in another department, take a class in something that interests you, or do something *really* out there like go back to school. Whatever it is, take the necessary steps so you know you're truly prepared to take a risk when an opportunity presents itself.

SUFFERING FROM JOB ATTENTION DEFICIT DISORDER: We know that we said it's normal to have up to eight jobs before age thirty-two, but your résumé is dicier than a dirty-water hotdog from a street vendor in New York City. (Believe us, dear reader. Unfortunately, we know what we're talking about.) Here's the thing about chronic job hopping: It can actually be a good thing *if* you're strategic about it, meaning you invest yourself in each position, build your skill set, and beef up your contacts, not to mention walk away and on to the next gig with a better idea of what you might want to do (and more important, what you *don't* want to do). On the other hand, if you phone it in for a few months only to quit because the learning curve started to get a little too, uh, curvy, or the powers-that-be denied your request to write off a weekend trip to Vegas for a bachelorette party (insert "Wooooooo!" here) as a business expense, then you're missing out on all the aforementioned benefits of moving around. Not to mention, you're kind of a brat.

UNEMPLOYED AND OVERWHELMED: Whether you were laid off yesterday, have been jobless for a while, or went all *Office Space* on the copy machine and received a security escort out of the building, being unemployed really sucks. If you've managed to squirrel away a decent safety net of savings, it might not seem so bad at first, especially if you hated your job. You sleep in, catch some matinee movies ($2 off tickets for shows before noon!), and take up decoupage. After about two weeks, though, your cozy little routine gets pretty old (how much *Judge Judy* can one girl watch?) and the absence of a paycheck makes you panic. You obsess over online job postings, hit up old contacts for leads, send out dozens upon dozens of résumés, and quickly realize that employers just aren't that into you. (Someday, scientists are going to discover a black hole that sucks in résumés submitted via HotJobs, Monster, and large corporate websites, along with other stuff that mysteriously goes missing, like socks from the dryer and phone numbers given out to guys at bars.) The job search can be demoralizing, and as the weeks and months of unemployment drag on, you start to dream up increasingly drastic ways to treat your wounded pride, culminating in the craziest of crazy fantasies: law school, a.k.a. the most expensive Band-Aid ever. (Step away from the *The PowerScore LSAT Logic Games Bible*. We repeat: Step away from *The PowerScore LSAT Logic Games Bible*.) At the risk of provoking you to unleash the type of fury that you usually reserve for office equipment (those court-mandated anger management classes didn't work so well, did they?), we'll offer some annoying words of advice that no job seeker wants to hear: Hang in there. You'll get through this. And, if you think that you're above getting a McJob to help pay the bills, guess what? You're not. Supporting yourself financially is, um, a really big part of being a grown-ass adult. It's not all fun and games, kittens and puppies, and rainbows and lollipops. After all, if it wasn't *work*, it would be called something else, like "not work," or "sipping Prosecco on the balcony of your Italian villa." (Full authors' disclosure here: That line is from our book *Friend or Frenemy?: A Guide to the Friends You Need and the Ones You Don't*. Yes, we just quoted ourselves. Because we can.)

Also, remember that nothing is permanent, and you are in charge of your career destiny. Plus, some sort-of bright news: A recent study from those über-smarties at Cambridge University shows that people who are laid off from work actually end up being better off mental-health-wise than those workers who were left behind to worry for an indeterminate amount of time about their future at the company.

GOING BACK TO SQUARE ONE: Congratulations! Despite self-doubt, fear of the unknown, and discouraging words from "concerned" family members and friends you've made the choice to become a student again/try out a completely new career/open your own dojo—whatever it takes to get your mojo working. On a positive note, you've managed to do what so many people talk about but never actually go through with: taking a risk in hopes that the payoff will be worth it. That's pretty damn cool. The bad news: The unknown can be pretty scary. Plus, if you're back in school, expect to have a bunch of anxiety nightmares that involve you showing up to class wearing nothing more than ankle socks and a mortified expression. Still, it's a small price to pay for following your dreams.

What's Really Going on When It Comes to Your Career: A Little Psychological Perspective

A quick note: Throughout Part Two of this book, you'll hear from Dr. Kevin Brennan, a licensed clinical psychologist concentrating on Young Professional issues, who will offer some reasons as to why you might be feeling turmoil during the redo-berty years. It's like free therapy—well, actually, it is free therapy if you borrowed this book from the library. It's merely really affordable therapy if you bought a copy of this book for you and all of your friends.

According to Dr. Kevin, we feel an existential panic of sorts in our early twenties as we try to figure out which career path to take. If we're lucky, we choose wisely and are able to find a fulfilling "happy" career. But this is a rare thing. Most of us make the wrong choice or worse: default into a career because we couldn't choose.

Fast-forward a few years, and the you-know-what hits the fan. "Yes, the seven-year itch is true and applies to relationships and careers," says Dr. Kevin. The next wave of existential panic grips us and we ask ourselves, Is *this* really it? "Today, this tends to happen by the late twenties and early thirties. Our parents had it at roughly forty-four," he adds.

Here's a little psychology lesson, courtesy of Dr. Kevin: The developmental phases of a career are widely regarded as the following: (1) exploration, (2) establishment, (3) maintenance, and (4) disengagement. Donald Super, the Great Oz of career psychology, suggested that we go through these four stages in succession. While his outdated theories need to be tweaked a little to account for our generation, they are still relevant in that we're feeling increasing pressure as we get closer to the "maintenance" stage of development.

"We've gone through all this time 'establishing,' but it's not really fulfilling. Now what? Blow all that time changing careers? Have a baby *now*? Maybe you can go back to school? Maybe you really need to just give up this lawyer gig and open a pastry shop. By the way, this actually happened and was well documented on the Food Network," says Dr. Kevin.

Yep, we've seen *Sugar Rush,* and the thought of it is making us hungry—or maybe having an existential crisis really works up an appetite.

If you haven't yet landed the gig of your dreams, don't worry. Whether you're pouring coffee or poring over case notes, running errands or running a business, you can and should take away something valuable from every job you've ever had. Hey, you never know. That next customer in line could end up being a valuable career connection, or one night, as you're counting out the money in your register, you could realize that you have a passion for accounting. Use every bit of an employment as a stepping-stone, a way to get closer to what you want out of a career.

Of course, just like there's no such thing as the perfect guy (or girl, for that matter), the perfect job doesn't actually exist. On a more touchy-feely note, keep this in mind: You are not your job, and you can and should find fulfillment and balance outside of the office—through your family, friends, hobbies, doing good deeds, and romantic relationships, to name a few very important things. (More on that later in the book.)

Adult Education: Experts Answer Your Most Burning Career Questions

If you're still feeling uncertain about your professional life, fear not! We've enlisted some savvy experts to help answer your most pressing career-related questions. (OK, so we didn't ask them this one: "How can I invent a ridiculous gadget that will allow me to cash in and spend the rest of my days living a life of leisure and profiting off the sales of my patented comfy blanket with sleeves, super-absorbent shammy, or whimsical singing bass?") Offering their invaluable insight are Penelope Trunk (founder of three startups, most recently Brazen Careerist, a social network to help young people manage their careers; the author of *Brazen Careerist: The New Rules of Success*; and a career columnist at the *Boston Globe*), Alexandra Levit (author of *They Don't Teach Corporate in College, How'd You Score That Gig?, Success for Hire*, and *New Job, New You*), and Dave Price (weather anchor on the CBS *Early Show* and all-around smart and inspiring guy).

Burning Question #1: I still have no idea what I want to do when I grow up. Any suggestions?

If only life were as easy as it was when you were a kid. You would watch in fascination as the checkout clerk scanned your mom's groceries and think, "Cool! This is what I wanna do when I'm a big girl!" There were no worries about job stability, benefits, or salary. Today, you're too big to ride around in the shopping cart at the supermarket, and making job-related decisions can be a complicated process. When it comes to figuring out what you want to do as an adult (which is, like, right *now*), Penelope Trunk tells it like it is. "Get over the idea that you're not grown up," she says. "Being a grown-up is about being lost. Kids are not lost. They have parents telling them what to do. You know you're an adult when you're lost."

Doing some homework can help you get orientated as you try to choose the right career for you. "Take time to do a self-assessment of your values, how you like to work, and what you'd be compelled to do even if you never got paid," Alexandra Levit suggests. She goes on to say that you should research careers and industries that map to your skills and interests. "Hit the Internet, set up informational interviews, take relevant coursework, and arrange to go on-site at organizations that sound interesting to you," she adds.

If you get lost while trying to find your way, don't worry, because that's all part of the journey. "It may take a series of changes before you hit your stride. You need fortitude for that," says Dave Price, who went into the television business in his late twenties. "Opportunity is a buffet; sample stuff, and if you don't like it, move on. But be sure that you really taste it. Invest yourself. Passions change and you need to figure out what your priorities are," he adds.

Burning Question #2: When it comes to priorities, which comes first: love or career?

It's a tried-and-true formula for countless romantic comedies. Take one successful yet "hardened" career woman, complete with a chic wardrobe, shiny hair, and a big apartment that no one could actually afford. Then, subtract a personal life, because said hardened career woman is too busy being recklessly ambitious to pursue any outside interests. Next, add in a major turning point where the hardened career woman finally realizes that she needs love—but there's a catch! She won't be able to get it until she overcomes a series of comical obstacles, which may or may not include obtaining a divorce from her high school sweetheart back in Alabama. In the end, the hardened career woman gets to quit her job, marry the man who sees through her icy exterior, and move to the country. The audience gets something else: a clear message that women who are very successful in their careers need to be rescued.

To make things even more confusing, at the same time that chick flicks are trying to melt our cold hearts, we're also given the opposite message: that we can have a career, family, and love all at once. But what happens when you're faced with a difficult choice? For example, what if you're working at a *job* you love, but the *person* you love is moving across the country? On one hand, you want career fulfillment and satisfaction, but on the other, when you're old, gray, and lying on your deathbed, you probably won't request the presence of your BlackBerry (or whatever device they'll come up with by then) to comfort you during your final hours. Now, for our own Carrie Bradshaw moment: When it comes to priorities, what comes first, love or career?

Once again, Penelope Trunk gives it to us straight. "A career does not make you happy. Relationships do," says Penelope. "A career enables you to have the stability you need to form relationships."

Unlike the "hardened" career woman stereotype from many a romantic comedy, you should strive for balance, suggests Dave Price. "Very few people get it all. The trick is to be happy with what you've got. And the key is not to enter into your thirties on a 'suicide mission' where you only go for one thing—love or career," he says. "You have to focus on both aspects of your life—professional and personal. When you have a vacation home, a car, and a boat, but no one to share it with, it sucks."

Alexandra Levit also touts a switch in attitude as you move into the next decade of life. "For the majority of people, I'd say career should come first in your twenties, and love in your thirties," she says.

"If you allow you career to be your number-one priority too far into your thirties, you may find yourself missing out on starting and raising a family, which is a major source of fulfillment for many people."

Burning Questions #3: Is it ever OK to quit a job without having another one lined up, even during a recession?

In this economy (are you tired of hearing those three words yet?) a new taboo has emerged: hating your job. Actually, there's an even bigger taboo: talking about hating your job. Don't get us wrong. Those of us who haven't been downsized, eliminated, laid off, or let go during these tough times feel thankful that we have gainful employment. However, just because you still have a job doesn't mean you get off easy. Remember the study from the brains at Cambridge who found that employees who survive layoffs are at greater risk of catching the crazies (our words, not theirs—surprise, surprise) than those who were let go. So the notion that you should blindly submit like a cult member to an abusive boss or a soul-sucking workplace is downright unhealthy and, worse, un-American. We're the land of the free, gosh-dangit, and we have an unalienable right to bitch about our jobs. No one can take that away from us. That being said, is it OK to quit a job without having a new gig lined up, even during a terrible recession?

According to our experts, it really depends. "It's usually best to stick it out until you get something better and are able to jump right into another position," says Alexandra Levit. "But if your work is seriously compromising your mental or physical health and it's torture to go into the office every day, you might not want to wait. After all, no job is worth sacrificing your well-being." She goes on to list scenarios that may warrant leaving now and worrying about the consequences later: You are being emotionally abused or sexually harassed; you have been asked to compromise your integrity; or you don't feel safe coming to work. (And while it's annoying when your boss asks you to add another chart to your PowerPoint presentation five minutes before a meeting, we doubt that your HR department considers that abuse.)

So unless you're being harassed, staying put is the best option. "You can have more power over your career and more choices if you stay in a job you hate," says Penelope. To make your life more tolerable for the time being, she suggests the following: Go to the gym during lunch. Don't work hard. Basically, do anything you need to do to cope with not quitting.

No, this isn't advice that they'd give you in school, but if you are in a truly desperate situation, you do what you need to do—within reason—to keep yourself sane. (The grass is always greener on the other side, and dealing with quickly eroding financial resources after you up and quit a job will also drive you batshit crazy.)

Burning Question #4: What's the plan of attack when you get laid off?

You knew that your company was downsizing, but you thought your job was safe. (Plus, no one else can figure out how to unjam the paper in the color printer.) After all, if they were going to cut people from your department, wouldn't they start with Christie, who's allergic to overtime and makes way more than you? But then one day while you're sitting at your desk updating your blog, you get an internal phone call. From HR. Crap. Thirty minutes later you're escorted out of the building, your dignity left behind with your laminated company photo ID and favorite coffee mug.

So now what? You can start by freaking out. No, really, go on a woe-is-me bender of booze (not too much, though—we don't want you to have to go to rehab), bad movies, and brownie mix. "Getting laid off is traumatic, but don't allow it to destroy your confidence," says Alexandra Levit.

Here's why: You're going to need that self-assurance when you look for a new job, which is something you need to do, like, now. "You should have no trouble landing on your feet provided you start looking for another job right away. Interviewers will appreciate your resilience, whereas they may become skeptical if you stay off the market for too long," she adds.

That's all well and good, but what happens when your severance package/unemployment runs out and the three hundred résumés you sent out have resulted in exactly zero callbacks? Brush up on your barista skills, says Penelope Trunk, since the new plan is to get a job at Starbucks. Seriously—they have good insurance. (Plus, we're addicted to the iced unsweetened green-tea lemonade.)

And while you're temporarily earning a living making Frappuccinos and those aforementioned tasty unsweetened green-tea lemonades, create—and execute—a personal project (it can be anything from writing a blog about your industry to starting your own company) that allows you to learn and grow, since that's the most important thing to do when you're job hunting, says Penelope. "Not only will it keep you sane and prevent you from having a gap in your résumé, but it'll give you something interesting to talk about on interviews and divert the conversation away from why you left your last job."

Burning Question #5: How do you handle an awful boss?

The devil wears Prada. Or, in your case, maybe she wears Ann Taylor or *he* rocks a mean pair of Dockers. No matter what clothing your boss prefers, though, he or she is making your life a nightmare. Passive-aggression, micromanaging, taking credit for your ideas—this is not your idea of a mentor. How do you deal with an inferior superior? Penelope Trunk offers this surprising advice:

"Want to deal with a bad boss? First, stop complaining. Unless your boss breaks the law, you don't have a bad boss; you have a boss you are managing poorly," she says. "Pick on your boss all you want, but if you were taking responsibility for your career, you wouldn't let your boss's problems bring you down.

Penelope goes on to say that you need to learn how to manage up. "Your job is not your job description. Your job is to make your boss's life easier. Find your boss's weaknesses and then graciously try to fill in so that your boss's performance improves," she says.

And, if you don't like it, you can always leave, because no one is forcing you to stay. Right? Don't let the door hit you in the booty on the way out. Yeah, that's what we thought.

Once you're able to effectively manage your boss and provide him or her with much-needed support, you'll get a lot more out of your relationship and maybe even some recognition for a job well done.

The Truth about Childhood Dream Jobs Exposed

As we mentioned earlier in the chapter, most little girls don't want to become a middle manager when they grow up. But had you pursued the profession you wanted as an eight-year-old, there's no guarantee that you would've fared much better. Here, we pull back the curtain and look at the reality of your childhood fantasy career.

	Princess	Singer	Supermarket Checkout Girl	Veterinarian	Astronaut
Qualifications (in your dreams)	Marrying a charming prince.	Remembering all the words to "Dress You Up" as you sing into a hairbrush and dance around your bedroom.	Looking cute in a blue vest.	Cleaning your hamster's cage and liberating frogs from their natural habitat.	Being good at science and knowing Saturn from Uranus.
Qualifications (in reality)	Marrying a slightly inbred prince.	Having that "It" factor, which in this case is barely-legal sex appeal, marginal talent, and incredible luck.	Possessing the remarkable self-control that prevents you from knocking out every person who tries to "sneak" (continued)	Graduating with a Doctor of Veterinary Medicine degree from a four-year program at one of the twenty- (continued)	NASA has only ever chosen 321 people to become astronauts, which means that the job requirements won't fit into this (continued)

	Princess	Singer	Supermarket Checkout Girl	Veterinarian	Astronaut
Qualifications (in reality) (continued)			forty-five items through the Express Lane.	eight accredited colleges of veterinary medicine. FYI: According to the latest stats, only one in three applicants are accepted to vet school, so hit the books, Dr. Dolittle.	tiny box. So let's just say there are a lot of them.
Job Duties (in your dreams)	Having pretty hair; wearing pretty dresses; being pretty.	Signing tons of autographs; performing in front of millions of adoring fans; wearing sparkly outfits and making out with	Using the scanner and getting to press all of the buttons on the cash register. How cool is that?!	Playing with newborn puppies, kittens, and bunnies all day, everyday.	Going where few men and women have gone before.

		your boy-band boyfriend.			
Job Duties (in reality)	Producing an heir to the throne; getting involved in countless charitable causes; enduring relentless media scrutiny about everything from your weight to your family life.	Publicly declaring your virginity; lip-synching in front of millions of tweens while struggling to keep up with your backup dancers (one of which is your future ex-husband).	Standing for long hours on your feet and dealing with crazy, coupon-wielding old ladies who want a third price check on those oranges.	Explaining to a distraught little girl that her beloved Puddles has gone to the big backyard in the sky. That and sticking your hand up a horse's ass if you're really lucky.	Going where few men and women have gone before . . . all while having to wear a diaper.
Compensation (in your dreams)	Living happily ever after.	Fame, fortune, and a friendship with Madonna.	You get to use the scanner and press all the buttons on the cash register. What more compensation do you need?!	Forest animals that love you so much they help you get dressed and clean your palace because you're a *princess* veter-inarian . . . duh.	An endless supply of astronaut ice cream— yippee!

	Princess	Singer	Supermarket	Veterinarian	Astronaut
Compensation (in reality)	A big advance to write a tell-all book detailing your very public divorce from the prince after he is caught playing "hide the family jewels with the nanny.	Fleeting fame; mountains of debt caused by bad management; a belief in Kabbalah, thanks to your friendship with Madonna (some dreams really do come true!).	Slaving away for minimum wage, only to lose your job to a self-checkout kiosk.	Vets in the U.S. make an average annual salary of $66,127, but getting bitten by a rabid dog or kicked in the head by an angry goat is priceless.	Currently, pay ranges from $65,140 to $100,701 per year, plus atrophied muscles.

IN CONCLUSION

Face it. We want to bang on the drums all night and party every day, but we can't, because we're grown-ups. Plus, we don't really have any musical talent outside of *Rock Band*. For many of us, the redo-berty years offer uncertainty when it comes to our professional lives. Big questions abound: Do we forge ahead on our current career path or try something totally new? How can we balance the demands of a job with the demands of, um, a life outside of that job? Does anyone actually read our résumés? (Scientists are getting closer and closer to discovering that black hole—we just know it.) And, is this all there is?

We wish we had all the answers, but we don't. Instead, we can offer a summary of the main points we just covered in this chapter. Think of it as a PowerPoint presentation, minus the slides and the cheesy clip art.

1. You are not your job.
2. Unless you have a big, fat trust fund, it's usually best to find a new job before you leave your current one. Of course, if you're stuck in a dangerous situation, by all means, make that leap without a backup plan in order to keep yourself safe and healthy. Besides these types of extreme situations, the following are not legitimate reasons for quitting a job without having another one lined up: (a) You're just not a morning person. (b) Work interferes with your social schedule, and frankly, that isn't very much fun. (c) Your boss tells you what to do, which automatically means that he or she has something against you. (d) Fluorescent lighting is very unflattering for a person with your coloring (you're an Autumn, by the way). (e) Your job is hard. (f) You hate the HR department and its fascist dress codes. (We live in America—since when is an exposed belly button a distraction?!)

3. If you don't like your career, try a new one. It's never too late.
4. In this economy. (We realize that this isn't a complete sentence. We just want to see how many times we can write "in this economy." So far, we're winning.)
5. Being a princess isn't all it's cracked up to be.

Money Talks: Some Financial Advice

We just finished talking about what you do in order to get money in the bank. Now, let's deal with saving and managing your dough. We asked personal financial expert Farnoosh Torabi, who wrote *You're So Money: Live Rich Even When You're Not* and appears on Soap-Net's series *Bank of Mom and Dad*, some burning questions about your wealth (or lack of it).

Burning Question #1: How do I know if I can afford to buy a house/apartment? Is there some sort of magical savings-to–down payment–to-mortgage formula?

FROM FARNOOSH: Your mortgage should not exceed 2.5 times your annual income. So if you earn $50,000 a year, avoid borrowing more than $125,000. Some banks may approve you for much more, but don't listen to them. All together, your monthly housing costs (mortgage plus insurance) should not exceed one-third of your monthly take-home pay. As for a down payment, aim to pay at least 15 percent to 20 percent of the asking price in cash. These days that's the norm—no more zero-money-down deals—and that's a good thing.

Beyond that, you also want to have extra savings in the bank, equivalent to six months living expenses to prove to the lender that you're financially stable and have a cushion to pay your mortgage in case you lose your job.

Bear in mind that home "affordability" is not just a mix of formulas and percentages. It's not about what you can afford today but also in the next several years. If you plan to change locations in a few years or need your savings for different goals like starting a business or going back to school, then buying a house today may turn into a financial burden down the road. Before purchasing a house, revisit your life goals. Think about where you want to be and what you want to do in the next five or so years.

Burning Question #2: How much should I really be saving for retirement?

FROM FARNOOSH: The short answer is this: more than you think. Realize you probably won't receive any social security benefits, at least not the way we're headed. The federal government's already made loud and clear that by 2037 we'll deplete the country's social security fund. On top of that, your health care is going to be a big expense. Not to forget, life expectancy is going up, too, so your money will need to last you a while.

My rule of thumb has always been, at least until your early thirties, contribute 10 percent of your salary to a 401(k). If you don't have a 401(k) through your employer, open an individual retirement account or IRA where you can (and should) put up to $5,000 a year. Be aggressive in the early years and get a bit more conservative as you get older and start a family. There are tons of online calculators that can give you ballpark estimates of how much you may need by sixty-five. Also don't rule out working during your retirement. Most aging baby boomers today say they plan on working or—get this—starting a business upon entering retirement.

Burning Question #3: Kinda creepy, but when should I put together a will?

FROM FARNOOSH: Don't freak out. People usually begin drafting their wills once they start a family or take on dependents. A will outlines how you'd like your assets to be distributed—who gets what. When you have a *who* (partner, kids, family) and a *what* (a house, a business, savings) in your life, then you should begin drafting a will. You can always revisit your will, which is a good idea since your life may change over time.

Burning Question #4: How can I deal with impulse spending? How much is too much for last-minute purchase?

FROM FARNOOSH: The same way you deal with impulse eating: distract yourself. Find a new hobby that takes your mind off "needing" a new pair of shoes or getting in the car and going to the mall. Instead, invite over a friend, go for a run, or clean out your closet and remind yourself of all the clothes you already have! It takes discipline, and you're allowed to cheat once in a while, just like with dieting. You can't go cold turkey forever. For that, give yourself a "shopping allowance" every month that's a small fraction of your take-home pay and only to be used after you've paid off all your monthly bills. Think of it like Weight Watchers points. If you don't use up your allowance in a week, you can roll over that money and save up for something great. But before any purchase, ask yourself, "Can I live without this?" Leave the item at the register for a day and see if you really crave it after distancing yourself from it. This has prevented a number of impulse buys for me over the years.

Burning Question #5: Should you pay off debt and student loans or save your money in an emergency fund?

FROM FARNOOSH: If you can do all at the same time, you're golden. Obviously, that's easier said than done. In a recession you need savings more than ever. I'd say that in dire economic circumstances you should make sure you do whatever you can to bulk up your savings before worrying about paying down all your debt. In most cases, though (not during a recession), you want to attribute at least 10 percent of your paycheck to savings (that includes retirement and emergency) and 20 percent or more to debt, depending on how much you owe and when you want to be debt free.

My other tip is to get a temporary side job to accelerate your payments toward debt or savings (as it may be). This is especially critical when you're young and your paycheck may not be enough to cover all your expenses.

[Authors' note: We can't stress enough how important it is to have some sort of an emergency fund, especially during the redoberty years. To put it bluntly, shit happens. Jobs get eliminated, cars break down, and teeth get cavities. If you simply don't have the money to cover the basics—especially if you have a bare-bones health-care plan or no insurance at all, young lady, and can't afford to fix a busted toof, broken bone, or, God forbid, something much worse—learn to live without those things that you would like to think are necessary but in reality are actually anything but. Need examples? Well, how about a daily caffeine jolt courtesy of a $4 latte or last-minute weekend escapes to Miami and Las Vegas with the girls? Being a grown-up is all about prioritizing. We have to say that one of the saddest things we've seen on television (with the exception of *Flavor of Love* and all of the spin-off shows it spawned) was the episode of *Sex and the City* when Carrie comes to the realization that she has wasted the equivalent to a down payment on her apartment on a closet full of fancy shoes. Even sadder is the fact that Manolo Blahniks are *so* seven years ago. You don't want to be that girl. Actually, we'd like to make a correction: You don't want to be that *woman*. Learn to separate your needs from your wants and understand that you won't actually die if you don't buy that latest it-whatever-thingy the magazines are hawking.]

Burning Question #6: When I was in my early twenties, from a cost standpoint, going out was easy. No one really had much cash, so we stuck with pizza and two-for-one beer specials. Now that I'm thirty, I find that there is much more financial diversity among my group of friends. While I have a modest assistant's salary, other people in my group bank some buck. How do I deal with socializing with friends who bring home the artisan bacon while I'm slaving away for Spam?

FROM FARNOOSH: I agree that by thirty there's a certain etiquette required to smoothly avoid pricey social indulgences, namely going out to eat at French restaurants with your six-figure-earning girlfriends when you're earning $35,000 (or much, much less) as a teacher. It's important not to forget that by now you're all technically adults, and you have goals and responsibilities. Saying you can't go to dinner because you're trying to be good and cook for a few months in order to afford a deposit on a new home or save up for a trip to Italy is totally acceptable—and won't make your friends think less of you. Maybe you'll actually inspire them.

That said being, sometimes you still want to enjoy life and go out with your friends. You're only human . . . and thirty. So, agree to meet for a drink or dessert instead of dinner and the whole shebang. No need to explain why you can't make it out for the full dinner, but if it comes up, explain that you have a ton of work to catch up on—hey, you are thirty and busy). My friend Michelle, as I wrote in *You're So Money*, did this most of the time. She rarely went out for full meals with friends. Instead she'd meet the girls around 9:30 or 10:00 for drinks, which is when the fun starts anyway. Or, if you *do* go for the whole evening's festivities and pay an arm and a leg for it, be prepared to make your breakfast, lunch, and dinner for the next five days to make up for it. Make concessions and stick to them.

My friends and I are also at a point in our friendships where it's cool saying things to each other like "That's way overpriced" or "That's not worth it." It's become code for "I'm not paying for that because I have no money!" So another bit of advice is be upfront with your friends. You don't have to spell out that you don't have the extra dough to order a $30 pasta dish (plus an app, plus wine, plus tip), but it's acceptable to say, "I can't spend that kind of money right now. I went crazy last month and I'm making up for it right now. But let me know if you'll be getting drinks or dessert afterwards. I'd be up for that!"

Sounding Off

From feeling like your body is staging a coup against you (how is it even possible that you're drunk from one glass of wine?) to comparing your life to everyone else's, there's no doubt that this stage of your life is filled with lots of angst, uncertainty, and frustration. At least you know that you're in good company. Here, our women answer the burning question: **What's the worst part of being in your late twenties/early thirties?**

"That college is over and the party kinda ended. Ha!"—*Lori, 30*

"Doing crazy things, dating crazy people, and wearing crazy outfits and *worrying* about what other people think."—*Carla, 27*

"My metabolism gets slower by the week, and sometimes I wake up with a sore back for no reason."—*Julie, 29*

"That damn biological clock! It's so stereotypical, and when I was in my twenties and heard about the clock I always thought, 'I won't feel that way, even if I'm not married.' But, it's not true. You know your childbearing years are limited and if you are stone-cold single you realize how *far* you are from having a kid."—*Laura, 32.5*

"Having to act like an adult, which means no more drunken antics without looking like an ass. When you were younger, it was funny, but now it's quite the opposite."—*Cheryl, 30*

"There are a lot of growing pains. Trying things out professionally and personally that may or may not fit and having to learn from those experiences, pick yourself up, and move forward."—*Mary, 30*

"Everyone is at a different stage. It used to be easy to relate and to feel 'normal,' and now I have to seek out people within my age group that are experiencing the same things I am."—*Brooke, 29*

"Your age makes you feel like you are supposed to have all of this figured out already. All of a sudden you find yourself questioning everything you thought you were so sure of."—*Melissa, 30*

"Feeling like you are not who you want to be yet. Waiting is horrible, and it's a petri dish for insecurities. And speaking of insecurities, this is the time when your metabolism starts slowing down and you get the little baggies under your eyes. Suddenly you realize that even though you're still 'young,' you are an ancient hag compared to Miley Cyrus."—*Jen, 26*

"Not making enough money. The appearance of fine lines and wrinkles."—*Sara, 28*

"The worst part is reaching that point when you realize your parents are just people. They went from being my close-to-flawless caretakers, always making sure everything was safe and easy for me, to flesh-and-blood, three-dimensional flawed beings."
—*Jamie, 26*

Five

Hooking Up, Shacking Up, and Marrying Up: The State of Your Love Life

CARRIE BRADSHAW: I couldn't help but wonder . . .

—from pretty much every episode of *Sex and the City*

RELATIONSHIP STATUS

Ah, love. It can move mountains, build bridges, keep us together, or tear us apart. It's a battlefield, a many-splendored thing, and a losing game. Essentially, love is the *Donnie Darko* of feelings: Anyone who brags, "I, like, totally get it man," is either full of crap or really, really high (or they watched the commentary on the DVD).

Now, just like we asked you to do in the career chapter, take yourself back to a simpler time. OK, so it won't be as innocent as your wide-eyed days spent idolizing the supermarket checkout girl and tweaking out on those Technicolor Pixy Stix. We're thinking more along the lines of when Britney was a virgin in real life, as opposed to just playing one on MTV. Back then, a relationship reached long-term status if it survived past homeroom, and boys and girls showed they cared by standing on opposite sides of the gymnasium during school dances. Courtship was simple—he passed you an origami-folded note in the cafeteria, and either you liked him (and circled "yes") or you didn't (and circled "no"). Of course, marriage and kids were a zillion million light-years away, a foregone conclusion once you reached Adult World, which isn't a sex toy emporium located off the side of the highway, you pervert, but a place where rules were made, fun went to die, and everyone spoke in trumpet notes, a la Charlie Brown's teacher.

The New Coming-of-Age Moments: The *Lovahs* Edition

Even though you checked off all the big "firsts" several years ago (otherwise you're a Drew Barrymore rom-com waiting to happen), when it comes to dating, love, and, yes, sexy time, sometimes it can feel like you're still a clueless preteen who assumed she'd get married before her twenty-fourth birthday and secretly thought that "sloppy thirds" was way gross.

Puberty	Redo-berty
Playing seven minutes in heaven	Getting down and dirty with a guy who only lasts seven seconds
Practicing French kissing on Buttons, your teddy bear	Taking care of business with "The Rabbit"
Going out of your way just so you can walk by his locker on your way to geometry class	Going out of your way just so you can walk by his desk on your way to a management training seminar
Looking for cute guys at the food court in the mall	Looking for cute guys at the Barnes & Noble in the mall
Getting groped by Daniel Goldberg while you slow dance to "Unchained Melody" at his bar mitzvah	Getting groped by Mr. Goldberg while you slow dance to "Unchained Melody" at his son's wedding
Going to the Warped Tour because the guy you like is a skater punk	Going to Coachella because the guy you like is a hipster

Puberty	Redo-berty
Writing your boyfriend's name on your notebook in permanent marker	Tattooing your husband's name on your ring finger
Getting a red velvet heart-shaped box of chocolates from your boyfriend for Valentine's Day	Getting a red velvet heart-shaped thong from your boyfriend for Valentine's Day
Driving by his house every night to see if his car is in the driveway	Checking his Facebook profile every night to track him via changes in his status update
Blasting "You Oughta Know" from your stereo after your boyfriend dumps you	Blasting "Since U Been Gone" on your iPod after your boyfriend dumps you
Sending your boyfriend a "143" message to his beeper	Sending your boyfriend a suggestive pic to his cell

Fast-forward those zillion million light-years (OK, more like fifteen regular years, because time magically moves faster than it used to). As an official resident of Adult World, you're older, wiser, and following a life plan that was accurately predicted by a game of MASH in sixth grade (or were we the only ones who played Mansion-Apartment-Shack-House?). Among the highlights: You're married to middle school heartthrob "Hot" Scott Sadowsky, reside in a Beverly Hills mansion, drive a red Corvette, work as a clothing designer, and, in a display of fertility that rivals the Duggar family, you spawned 12 kids. Everything worked out exactly as planned, right? Um, not quite. In case you somehow missed all ten seasons of *90210*, where Kelly Taylor abused diet pills, got burned in a fire, joined a cult, developed a coke addiction, overcame said coke addiction (but was almost killed by a fellow rehab patient in the process), attracted a stalker, suffered a miscarriage, became a single mom, and, in what was arguably the most disturbing thing to happen to her, ended up working as guidance counselor, life has this funny way of taking people to unexpected places.

In reality, "Hot" Scott Sadowsky went on to attend a Big 10 school, where he continued his streak of dating the hottest cheerleader on the squad—although, after some good old-fashioned college experimentation, he realized that he preferred the boys at the bottom of the pyramid, if you catch our drift. After you graduated with a BFA in something not very useful and got an advanced degree in several failed relationships, you reunited with Scott thanks to the beauty of Facebook, when you both realized that you were looking for roommates. (Scott needed a living-situation downgrade after his dad refused to bankroll his not-so-budding acting career, and you lost your sweet, sunny one-bedroom in a bad breakup but, on a positive note, gained sole custody of Al Roker, the ten-year-old rescue cat from the SPCA that you shared with your good-for-nothing asshole ex-boyfriend who was cheating on you with a twenty-two-year-old who works as a receptionist at a spa and sports a wonky eye.) Together, in a cramped apartment, you, Al Roker, and "Hot" Scott live as woman, cat, and Best Gay, till death, or legalized same-sex marriage, do you part. (As for children, you do get to experience the beauty of pregnancy a few years down the road, when Scott and his husband, Blake, declare their undying love for your eggs.)

All right, so maybe you can't relate to the touching love story of a woman, her best gay, her desirable uterus, and her arthritic cat, but we're trying to show you that life—especially anything involving romantic intrigue—takes unexpected turns as you get older. It doesn't matter if you're single and ready to mingle or coupled and ready to Netflix, because the redo-berty years bring about agony and ecstasy when it comes to matters of the heart.

Now, without further ado, let's examine several possible states of your love life right now.

Some Likely Scenarios: Where You're at with Your Love Life

ONE . . . SINGULAR SENSATION: Let's get the crazy talk out of the way right now. If you're single, it doesn't mean you're a girl gone wild, an incomplete person, a cat lady in training, or a pet project for well-meaning yet misguided friends, family members, and colleagues who think they can "fix" you by fixing you up on a series of dates that will inevitably result in more uncomfortable silences than an episode of *The Hills*. And, not to rain on your parade, but your having to check the "single" box when you fill out forms at the doctor's office doesn't automatically make you fun, flirty, and fabulous, either. (You go, girl!) Since we prefer advice that isn't totally insulting or condescending, here's how we look at it: Being unattached to a romantic partner once you hit your late twenties or thirties and beyond—oh, the horror!—doesn't mean that you automatically stop being *yourself* and, instead, morph into a sad, baby-desperate spinster.

During your redo-berty years, the haze of weddings tends to over-shadow the fact that life isn't a fairy tale, and just as people get married for different reasons, they also have their own reasons for not being married. So, whether you haven't found the right person yet or you shudder at the thought of till death do us part, love your life as it is, own it, and whenever that yenta from accounts payable says she knows a "nice boy" who would be perfect for you (translation: he's thirty-eight, lives with Mom not because he has to but because he likes to, and sews jackets out of human skin in his spare time), shut her down with this reply: "Is he packin'?"

BLINDSIDED BY A BREAKUP: "Sometime surprise life give you" read the awkwardly translated fortune that came with the moo shu pork lunch special you wolfed down in record speed last week. Little did you know that the "surprise life give you" would be the accidental discovery of "{craigslist casual encounters m4m}" in the browser history on your live-in boyfriend's computer. (Sorry, but we're on a roll after the "Hot" Scott story.) With the click of a mouse, you realized that you could never be man enough for your man, and your future, which had once seemed so bright and clear, was now hazier than the smoke and Acqua Di Gio–filled air at your friendly neighborhood gay bar.

No matter who initiates a breakup or what causes the split— infidelity, uncertainty, or insanity—it's always traumatic when a relationship implodes. And you can up the devastation factor from "bring on the Chubby Hubby" to "bring on the men in white coats" if said relationship was one of those serious kinds where you shared an address, a last name, or the same strain of genital herpes. Give yourself ample time to wallow (that means months, not years) then delete the "Ten Best Breakup Songs" playlist from your iTunes library, buy a fancy new push-up bra, and get your hot single ass back out there. And by "out there," we mean sign up for an online dating site because that's what all the single kids are doing these days. (Just make sure that you Photoshop your profile picture. No guy is going to ask out the girl with a nasty case of red eye.)

NOT THE MARRYING KIND (AT LEAST, NOT FOR NOW): Our society has this annoying little habit of painting women as desperate, deranged, overbearing basket cases who will stop at nothing— and we mean nothing—to drag their helpless insignificant others across the finish line in the race of life: the big-ass rock, an elaborate wedding, matching place settings, 2.5 kids, and a we-mail account (jennyheartsjosh@vomit.com). But what if—in an M. Night Shyamalan plot twist—*you* are the one who isn't ready to commit? (And what if you're a ghost, too?!) See, in a place called Realityville, some women either aren't ready or aren't sure they ever want to sign up for better or worse (especially that "for richer or poorer" business). It's perfectly normal (and incredibly sane) to not want to get married for the *wrong* reasons, which include but aren't limited to: you want to have a baby, one of you needs a green card, he stands to inherit the throne, or you're turning thirty and everyone else you know is hitched. It's also OK to be truly content with the way things are in your relationship and not need a piece of paper to validate it.

COUPLES' CRUISE CONTROL: You and your boyfriend have been dating for so long that he remembers when you got your belly button pierced on spring break and you can barely fit one leg into the slutty Bebe dress you wore to his fraternity formal senior year. For a while you were fine with the state of your non-union. No, really, you were. You shrugged off the prying questions from every coworker, great-aunt, and hair stylist about when you were getting married, and you were genuinely happy to don a bridesmaid dress—all six times. But as the years creep by and the wedding invitations continue to overtake your mailbox, you can't help but wonder when it would be your turn to change your Facebook relationship status to "Engaged" (don't pretend like you're not going to do it).

First, you give him a subtle nudge by taping a picture of a two-carat, cushion-cut diamond on the fridge next to a Post-it note with your ring size, assuming that he'll be abso-freaking-lutely thrilled by how easy you're making it for him to empty his entire savings account on a piece of jewelry just because De Beers told you so. After a few months of waiting for him to propose, you start to question if you've been wasting your time in a dead-end relationship all these years. And after a few more months of waiting for him to propose, you have a meltdown at the wedding of two people who met last year. On the Internet.

You're stuck in couples' cruise control. For advice on how to deal with this unpleasant situation see Intermission #6: Stuck in Relationship Limbo: To Marry or Not to Marry, That Is the Question. And, lest you think that we're anti-woman, of course you could be the one who isn't sure if you want to get married. Like, duh. Make like a Mad Lib and reread this scenario, only substitute your boyfriend's name where you are mentioned. (OK, so we highly doubt he has a belly ring, wore a Bebe dress to your formal senior year, or took a walk down the aisle six times as a bridesmaid, but you get the gist.)

LIVING HAPPILY EVER AFTER: Congratulations on finding your soul mate/life partner. Now you can get started on your true calling in life: making babies! We kid, we kid (pun sort of intended). But seriously, when are you going to have a baby? And, if you already have a child, when are you going to have another one, because we're sure that Emma would love a little brother or sister to keep her company? (We're just trying to show you that the annoying personal questions don't stop once you get married.)

What's Really Going on When It Comes to Your Love Life: A Little Psychological Perspective

Sure, there are obvious reasons why love causes so much anxiety during the redo-berty years. First of all—and we guess this applies to people of all ages—*amore* favors pheromones and, more important, *feelings* over logic and reason. Everyone knows that the *F* word can lead to good stuff (hugs, kisses, and warm fuzzies) or turn ugly in a jiffy (restraining orders, paternity tests, and irreconcilable differences). The redo-berty years are also a time when the coupled among us grapple with uncertainty about their relationships, commitment issues, and thoughts of forever, if ever, and never. For the single ladies (by the way, we're going to focus mostly on you during this chapter—sorry, partnered-up peeps), there's that whole longing-for-companionship-and-fear-of-being-alone thing that goes along with being human. Throw in the biological clock (you know we just had to get that in there), along with the societal and/or family pressure to pair up and "settle down" even if you're completely happy with your life as it is, and we have a recipe for the type of heartburn that Alka-Seltzer won't alleviate.

In order to understand the less obvious reasons for angst during the redo-berty years, we need to dig a little deeper. For that, we turn to our doctor-on-call, Dr. Kevin Brennan. As we mentioned at the beginning of the book, we're currently experiencing the same sort of life reevaluation that our parents' generation did during middle age. Why is this happening now, you might be asking? According to Dr. Kevin, in short, it's because our parents did a really good job. (FYI: When he speaks of "our parents," he is referring to the typical parents of this generation in terms of the majority socioeconomic status.)

"Our parents gave us the best they had to make sure we had the options for the most fulfilling life possible," Dr. Kevin explains. "They gave us the space we needed, the knowledge we needed, the lack of commitment we needed, the 'time to think it over' we needed, and the self-centered values we needed. They swapped out all expectations for one: to do what will make us happy."

Waaaah, waaaah, poor us, right? But Dr. Kevin knows his stuff. Expecting happiness without hardship is totally unrealistic and extremely stressful. Plus, even if you childhood bore more of a resemblance to *Mommie Dearest* than *Father Knows Best*, think about our unrealistic expectations. The goal of reaching perfection permeates our society, from television and movies to advertising and magazines. One example involves a modern-day fairy tale of sorts: the celebrity holy union and subsequent motherhood—or, for the really progressive starlet, the baby bump and the seemingly committed relationship with the person reportedly responsible for said baby bump (because the couple doesn't plan to tie the knot until same-sex marriage is legal in every state). We seem to love nothing more than the story of a bad girl gone domestic, a pregnant former party animal glowing from the pages of *In Touch Weekly*, her body finally reaching a "healthy" size four in the third trimester, those nights filled with dancing on tables and, er, powdering her nose far behind her. She's beaming with happiness and "over the moon." Come to think of it, we would be too if companies gave us a bunch of really expensive shit just for getting knocked up. (You don't think they actually buy those cashmere diapers, platinum baby rattles, and $1,500-dollar strollers, do you?)

Unlike previous generations, we've been conditioned to search for and expect this perfect happiness—to chase the over-the-moon feeling that our parents sacrificed so much for. This feeling that we deserve a perfect union makes the search for love that much more intense. According to Dr. Kevin, those expectations can provide relationship problems for a woman who is looking to start a family and find "the One" during these years. For practical reasons, the One has to be ready to settle down and also has to be someone who earns enough money to make a "stay-at-home" situation possible or at least be able to afford day care. (Authors' interjection: We don't necessarily agree with this part, but we totally see his point.) Finding the One also entails landing a great guy—"someone who is not a jellyfish but also not an asshole (rare, indeed)."

True dat, Dr. Kevin. True dat.

Adult Education: Experts Answer Your Five Most Burning Love Questions

Trying to narrow down the most burning love questions was quite a feat—kind of like trying to chose a favorite episode of *The Golden Girls*. If you're single and loving it, go on with your bad self, girlfriend! And, if you're coupled and content, go one with your bad selves, girlfriend and boyfriend (or wife and husband, girlfriend and girlfriend, wife and wife—we don't discriminate). So we decided to focus on all the single ladies out there who are having a hard time finding Mr. Right, let alone Mr. Right Now.

We get by with way more than a little help from our expert friends: Rachel Greenwald, dating coach, matchmaker, and *New York Times* bestselling author of *Why He Didn't Call You Back: 1,000 Guys Reveal What They Really Thought About You After Your Date*; Kristina Grish, relationship expert and author of several books including, most recently, *The Joy of Text: Mating, Dating, and Techno-Relating*; and Justin Prugh, writer for Askmen.com

And for those of you who are unhappy in your relationships, there's always Ashley Madison—you know, that creepy website with a name that curiously sounds like an American Girl doll and the motto, "Life is short. Have an affair." Now hit it, Beyoncé: "All the single ladies / Now put your hands up / Wuh uh oh uh uh oh uh oh oh uh uh oh!"

Burning Question #1: Let's just get this one out of the way: Why didn't he call you?

You know the drill: Your friend sets you up with her boyfriend's coworker, whom we'll call Mike (because everyone has gone out with a Mike). You meet for drinks and are pleasantly surprised to find that Mike is not as short, fat, bald, or cross-eyed as you anticipated. After two rounds and a decent amount of witty banter, he kisses you good night (on the cheek).

You're hesitant to use the C word, but you really think there was a *connection* (cue the "most dramatic rose ceremony ever" music from *The Bachelor*). You wait to hear from him, but nothing. Nada. Not even a lousy text. We could tell you that he's just not that into you, but something (estrogen, perhaps?) forces us to ask, "*Why* is he just not that into you?" Beats the hell out of us, so we asked the ultimate expert: Rachel Greenwald.

According to Greenwald's data (based on one thousand in-depth "exit interviews" with guys), men make quick (and often incorrect) assumptions about your personality based on small comments or gestures you make during a date (like interrogating the waiter about how the fish is cooked or trying to pick up the check). And if he doesn't like the picture he's painted of you, he won't call you. Of course it's unfair, and no one is telling you to pretend to be someone you're not. The idea is to first figure out how your dates perceive you and learn how to avoid being stereotyped. Basically, hide all your flaws until he's madly in love with you or, even better, wait until you're pregnant with his lovechild! In all seriousness, if you *really* want to know why a guy who you thought you'd hit it off with didn't call you and are looking for legit, actionable advice—as opposed to the kind your mom or gay hairstylist gives—read her book. (By the way, we asked a guy and he said, "The obvious and tragic answer is that he doesn't like you, at least not as much as you like him." Obviously that was unacceptable, so he added, "Or, if it'll help you sleep at night, he's gay.") That's more like it. But seriously, if he doesn't call you, move on.

Burning Question #2: Where's the best place to meet men? Have you tried a sports bar? We hear there are tons of hot, single, employed men just waiting for a woman such as you to save them from yet another dull evening of beers and basketball with the guys. In the hopes of *not* getting that as an answer, we first consulted Justin Prugh, a real live dude. His suggestion, while general, is a good starting point:

Do things you enjoy outside the walls of your home with like-minded people. "The chances of meeting a guy you like go way up when you have something meaningful in common," he says. "Plus you're comfortable when you're in your element and therefore most attractive."

Relationship expert and author Kristina Grish agrees. "The best way to meet a man is to put yourself in situations in which you naturally shine," she says. "Just spend more time in environments that are conducive to an organically positive first impression and less in situations that make you fidget, cause you to try too hard, and encourage you to wear clothes that tug in all the wrong places." For most people, that rules out bars.

So where else can you meet men? Rachel Greenwald has plenty of clever suggestions that can suit ladies with all sorts of interests and personality types. Here, in her own words, she shares them:

1. **On Facebook:** Finding great guys is all about networking through your friends, so scroll through the friends lists of your Facebook friends and play "I Spy a Cute Guy." If you spy someone intriguing, ask your mutual friend if he's single (or check his relationship status if his profile isn't private) and ask to be introduced. Because this isn't an official online dating site, the pressure is off. You can get to know each other first as friends while eliminating Internet safety worries since you have a mutual acquaintance.

2. **On Twitter:** Send a tweet Friday afternoon that you're meeting friends at your favorite pub or café, and say you're looking forward to anyone joining you for a spontaneous happy hour. Tell your "followers" to bring their friends. You're bound to meet new people, and even if they're not single, they might know someone to fix you up with later.

3. **Off-beat, niche online dating sites:** If you're tired of seeing the same profiles that don't meet your standards on those big online

dating sites, don't give up on online dating all together. Try a smaller site with a unique twist. Here are some sites where my clients have met: www.gk2gk.com ("geek to geek": think Bill Gates!); www.intellectconnect.com (brainy singles); www.datemypet.com (pet lovers); and www.bbwpersonalsplus ("big, beautiful women and their admirers"). Find more by Googling "online dating" + your niche or interest.

4. **At your own "recycling" party:** You definitely know interesting men who aren't right for you but might be right for someone else (perhaps your single brother, dentist, cousin, coworker, or former date?). Host your own party and "recycle" these men by inviting single women to come with a single guy whom they'd recommend to other women.

5. **Teach your own man-class:** Contact your local adult education center and offer to teach a seminar geared toward men. Identify something you can do that men typically can't, and watch guys sign up in droves. One of my clients created a cooking class called "Bachelors: Learn How to Cook Ten-Minute Meals." She wasn't a great chef herself, but she collected five super-simple recipes (mostly out of canned food!) and soon had twenty-five single men sitting in front her as she taught the ninety-minute class. She reported that three men asked her out later that night, and two of them were *really cute!*

6. **Join a Meetup.com Group:** Meetup.com offers a unique, social way to connect with people in your town around mutual interests. If you go to www.meetup.com and search for something like "Singles in Detroit who love puggles" or "Singles in Denver who love to travel," you'll find dozens of like-minded groups who gather regularly to merge their hobbies or passions with their search for a mate.

7. **Having coffee with women:** Next time you walk into a party, don't

scan the room for a tall, handsome man but rather seek out the most social, outgoing *woman* you can find. Get to know her, invite her for coffee next week, and brainstorm how to fix each other up with a great guy you each know who's not right for you. Women are natural matchmakers, and coffee with an outgoing woman can be a fabulous gateway to a great guy.

Burning Question #3: What are the biggest dating mistakes single women make? (And yes, men make plenty of mistakes, but we're not talking about them right now, are we?)

According to Rachel Greenwald, single women have a habit of trying to figure out "who someone really is" on a first date. This doesn't work, she says, because initial encounters (first dates, flirting at a party, exchanging emails through an online dating site) are always artificial since we are never our true selves in the beginning; we might be nervous, or overeager, or cynical, or keeping up our guard, or maybe drinking too much. The point is that first impressions are always based on a stereotype of the kind of person you *think* someone is, which is rarely accurate. That's why she's an advocate of the the Three-Date Rule: Always go on three dates (as long as he seems like a "nice enough" guy) before deciding if there's real potential. If you can get past the initial encounter to the second and third date (and beyond), only then can you both begin getting to know who each other really is.

Now we're going to tell you what our TG (Token Guy), Justin Prugh, said, but you have to promise not to get mad at him because he's only being honest. Swear? Okay, then, here goes nothin': "Sadly, there are many big no-nos to choose from, including coming on too strong, talking about long-term commitment too early, being clingy or overprotective, hitting on his friends." (Authors' note: Really? Who's actually hit on his friends?) But the boo-boo that seems to trump all others is the discussion of a previous boyfriend. "Guys are so not interested in anything about him and will most likely default to interpreting even a mention of his existence, regardless of context, as you having baggage," Justin says. So while you might think it's absolutely crucial for your date to know that you were thisclose to getting engaged but your ex had commitment issues and blah, blah, blah, keep that info between you and your therapist.

Burning Question #4: I hate dating. How can I enjoy it more? Well, with that attitude it's no wonder you haven't found yourself a nice fellow. Sorry, we don't mean to sound like your great aunt Ruth (who loads up her purse with sugar packets and coffee creamers every time she eats at Denny's), but going on a date shouldn't feel like getting a wisdom tooth yanked, and even if it does get exhausting and demoralizing at times, don't let him see you sweat, or grimace for that matter. Here's why: Your attitude can become a self-fulfilling prophecy in turning away guys who may end up surprising you later with romantic potential, says Rachel Greenwald. Remember those one thousand single men she questioned? Well, one of the top ten reasons they cited when asked why they didn't call you back is the "Debbie Downer Syndrome," meaning women who acted pessimistic or cynical or did more than their share of complaining. This syndrome can emerge in subtle ways, such as when a man says you look nice and you reply, "You probably say that to everyone." So frankly, even if you have to fake an upbeat attitude when you're on a first date, do it.

It also might help to manage your expectations, says Kristina Grish. "Stop wondering if every guy is 'the One,' which is what we all do until we meet *him*." Instead, think of dating as gathering info on traits you like and don't like in a man and potential life partner, and some of the stress will lift. If you realize that a guy's not for you, use the date as an opportunity to make a new friend, network for a new job or a new client, or expand your knowledge on a new subject, like *Star Trek*.

In order to make dating less awkward for you, Rachel offers these ideas for keeping the conversation flowing: Come prepared to discuss your favorite topics—books, travel, music, whatever—or pepper him with questions that can help you find the right guy going forward. Where does he meet great singles in your town? Is he a member of any fun groups? Is he going to any interesting events in the near future? "Little tidbits he reveals may lead you to the spot where your future husband is waiting," she says. "Or simply go for the good karma and offer to fix him up with a friend of yours who might make a better match—there's someone for everyone!"

Burning Question #5: But come on, is there really someone for everyone?

Do you want to know if there's really a God, too? Well, there is and apparently she looks like Alanis Morissette. A wise woman (okay, Andrea's grandmother) once said, "There's a lid for every pot," and our experts unanimously agree that there is indeed someone for everyone. In fact, Kristina Grish and Justin Prugh both said that there are many, many people for everyone (Justin even kindly pointed out that bisexuality doubles your chances). And if you're the type who needs cold hard numbers to be convinced, consider this: Rachel Greenwald has been responsible for 712 marriages . . . and counting.

In order to make things easier for you, we decided to break down our experts' answers into a mini-panel discussion of sorts. Enjoy!

KRISTINA: AI think there are many people for everyone, and where we are in our life at the moment—and what we want from our lives in the future—determines whether the person we're with, at that point in time, is the one we stay with forever. You also have to be open in a way that means you're more forgiving of flaws and welcoming of change. Compromise isn't just meeting in the middle; it's literally compromising what you want to get to a happier place. You have to really know yourself and know what you want from life to find out where control ends and new priorities begin.

JUSTIN: There is certainly someone for everyone. In fact, there are many, many people for everyone. Incompatibility happens, but odds are overwhelmingly in favor of the fact that you'll mesh nicely with one of the 3 billion or more guys around. And if not, bisexuality doubles your chances. (Thanks again for that one, Justin!)

RACHEL: Absolutely! I've been responsible for 712 marriages so far. I have seen the most surprising connections. The one and only common denominator among all these marriages was that the wonderful mate someone found came in a *completely different* package than what he or she was looking for. My clients and readers observed that they were initially looking for mostly objective traits (e.g., education, height, job, religion, certain interests, etc.), but when they found love, it was the subjective traits (e.g., intelligence, humor, kindness, generosity, etc.) that sparked and sealed their connection. There is someone for everyone if you are open to finding a mate with the subjective traits that truly matter in the long run.

MASH (for Realists)

The last time you played this future-predicting game (circa 1992 during Mrs. Cabrera's social studies class), the results had you living in a mansion in Hawaii with your husband, Steve Urkel; cruising around town in a white Ferrari (the most practical mode of transportation for your twelve children); and enjoying a lucrative career in teaching. So maybe fortune-telling capabilities of MASH fall somewhere between Miss Cleo and a Magic 8 Ball, but that won't stop us from tearing out a piece of paper from our old notebook (the one with the unicorn jumping over a rainbow) and creating MASH 2.0.

Who You Marry (Ahem, Whom You'll Marry)

1. The random dude you hooked up with last Saturday
2. That asshole ex-boyfriend who broke your heart
3. Ted, your office's creepy IT guy
4. "Luv269" on Match.com
5. Angelina Jolie (*Surprise!* You're a lesbian!)

Your Ring

1. Classic two-carat Tiffany solitaire
2. "He went to Jared!" half-carat chip on a gold band
3. The finest the gumball machine had to offer
4. A tattooed band (how very Pam and Tommy)
5. The six-carat pink diamond monstrosity Ben gave J.Lo

Your Wedding Dress

1. A tasteful white pantsuit
2. A custom-made Vera Wang confection
3. A white string bikini (keepin' it classy!)
4. A replica of the dress Stephanie Seymour wore in the "November Rain" video (Google image search it now)
5. A "You'll love David's Bridal" number (with lots and lots of rhinestones)

Where You Live

1. A Winnebago
2. His parents' basement
3. You split your time among your four homes
4. A cul-de-sac in New Jersey
5. A gated community in the O.C.

Number of Children

1. None . . . that you know of
2. Eight (thanks to an overzealous fertility doctor)
3. One* (the asterisk is because "Hot" Scott and Blake's daughter Mia shares your genes, but calls you "Aunt")
4. Nineteen and counting (you're trying for your own reality show)
5. Two (someone reading this has to be normal)

Your Job

1. "Freelancing" (a.k.a. unemployed)
2. Dental hygienist
3. Starbucks barista
4. Stay-at-home mom
5. CEO of a Fortune 500 company

His Job

1. Stay-at-home dad
2. Televangelist
3. Investment banker
4. Urologist
5. Walmart greeter

Your Car

1. A tricked-out minivan
2. A practical Honda Civic
3. Public transportation
4. A gas-guzzling SUV that no one really needs outside the wilds of Alaska
5. A high-status piece of European engineering that you drive in an (unsuccessful) attempt to convince others that your marriage is a happy one

IN CONCLUSION

Love sure ain't easy for anyone, but it's especially tough during the redo-berty years, a time when we're conditioned to expect Happy! Happy! Joy! Joy! (damn those glowing couples in the J.Crew catalog) but often get a dose of reality instead. And we're not just speaking to those of you who are still searching for Mr. Right or, if you've found him, waiting *very, very* patiently for a proposal (we hear that cutting out pictures of engagement rings and taping them all over his apartment works like a charm). Married people experience their fair share of relationship drama, too. How else do you explain *Wife Swap,* couples therapy, and the dismal divorce rate (almost 50 percent and rising)? Maybe the secret to all of this love stuff lies in our expectations, since the older we get, the harder it is to predict what the future has in store for us. So for example, instead of obsessing over "happily ever after," we should be thinking more like "happy for right now."

In the meantime, here are the main points that you should take away from this chapter (please write these down in your composition notebook because there will be a test later in the week).

1. Sure, everyone has stories of awkward first dates, but if you think of dating as on par with Chinese water torture, that negative attitude might be a self-fulfilling prophecy.
2. If you want to meet someone new, get off your bum! The chances of finding a guy you like improve greatly if you have something meaningful in common.
3. Stop writing your first name with the last name of every cool guy you meet on the front of your Trapper Keeper.
4. Our experts all agree that there is indeed someone for everyone. (Sorry to break the bad news, but you're not that unique. And—this will really blow your mind—you're not perfect either!)
5. All the single ladies: Put your hands up!

Stuck in Relationship Limbo:
To Marry or Not to Marry, That Is the Question

You've been asking (okay, harassing) your boyfriend about getting engaged for months and all he can do is mumble some crap about the fact that the world is going to end on December 21, 2012, so why even bother spending all this money on a wedding when we're going to vaporize, anyway? (He's been watching too many Armageddon specials on The History Channel.) Or maybe he's the one who's tried to initiate the "talk," but you're experiencing doubts about happily ever after. Before you go and drop the "by this time next year . . ." bomb on him or start believing into any apocalyptic hype, allow us to introduce you to Andrea Passman Candell, who wrote the oh-so-appropriately titled book *His Cold Feet: A Guide for the Woman Who Wants to Tie the Knot With the Guy Who Wants to Talk About It Later.* She's here to talk you off the relationship limbo ledge and offer advice on dealing with his (or your) marriage issues.

Burning Question #1: We've been in a committed relationship for years, so why is he so freaked out about getting engaged?
FROM ANDREA: Two people can be ready for something at different times. It's very common for a woman to feel ready to get married before her boyfriend. There's a gender difference here. When women think of marriage, most think of family and togetherness. When men think of marriage most think ball-and-chain (charming, right?).

Don't take his hesitation personally. His not popping the question might not have anything to do with you. He could be dealing with his own fears, fears that have to do with change and the unknown. (What if we don't get along in five years? What if there's someone else out there more perfect for me?) All of this anxiety can come along with a normal engagement process.

Burning Question #2: What's the best way to have "the talk"?

FROM ANDREA: Instead of nagging him and dropping not-so-subtle hints, schedule a time to sit down with your boyfriend to have a discussion about how each of you feel about getting engaged. During the chat share how you feel about the status of your relationship and talk about what's making you feel ready to move this relationship forward. Get a sense as to how he feels. Stay on target by sharing your feelings and experience rather than focusing on a timeline. Determine if you both have the same hopes for your relationship and whether you both want it to move forward.

Burning Question #3: Should you give him an ultimatum?

FROM ANDREA: If you mean something along the lines of, "You better propose by March or else," then definitely not. (Authors' note: Screaming and crying like a child who just had her blanky taken away is so *not* attractive.) In fact, the person you should be giving an ultimatum to is yourself. Set a timeframe for how long you're willing to stay in the relationship without the type of commitment you want. Once you call the shots and make a decision to do what's good for you, then you'll feel empowered.

It's okay to let him know where you stand. ("I love you and I would love for us to get married. But since marriage is important to me, I'm telling you that at some point, if we're still not engaged, I'm going to have to move on.") This gives him the opportunity to make his own decision as to what he wants to do instead of making him feel like he's being told what to do.

Burning Question #4: What to do if you're the one who isn't ready to move forward?

FROM ANDREA: The advice goes both ways, whether it's for a man or for a woman. Consider your feelings about marriage and your relationship. Determine if it's just cold feet or something else that's cause for concern. When it's cold feet, the jitters stem from feelings about marriage itself (what if we don't get along in ten years, what if we get divorced, etc.). When a red flag is in the picture, the feelings are focused on some dynamic of the relationship (I often don't feel good in this relationship, we don't have the same values, etc.). It's a matter of knowing what needs improvement and what's a deal breaker.

Six

WebMD Doesn't Count as Your Primary Care Physician: Personal Health and Fitness

The secret of staying young is to live honestly, eat slowly, and lie about your age.

—Lucille Ball

LET'S GET PHYSICAL, PHYSICAL!

Hopefully you're sitting down, because we're about to drop a bomb that's more earth-shattering than when you found out that Milli Vanilli weren't really singing and Cyndi Lauper's "She Bop" was actually an ode to touching your "no-no spot." The big reveal is this: Right now, you're older than you've ever been. (See, we told you it was *major*.) Want to know something else that's quite revolutionary? Getting older is only natural, because we're living organisms, and aging is kind of, like, our *thing*.

It all seems logical enough, unless, of course, you believe everything you watch on TV, see in the movies, and read in magazines. Thanks to advertisements for miracle moisturizers, reality shows dedicated to MILFs, and visions of Madonna's ridiculously buff arms, aging women now seem about as natural as, say, injecting a botulism-related neurotoxin into your face. Case in point: Baby-faced actresses will always grace magazine covers, but today what really sells supermarket tabloids are actual babies, or, even better, baby bumps. Yep, our obsession with youth has brought us to the dawning of the Age of the Underage, a fascinating time in history when you can make headlines as a zygote and become a has-been before you've even left the womb via a C-section that was scheduled months in advance so that your famous mommy could immediately get back to work showing up on red carpets at the opening of an envelope.

In a culture where Tayor Swift is just about ready for her AARP card, what's a grown-ass woman to do? Well, you could hit up eBay and put in a bid on a hyperbaric chamber, or you could get a grip and accept that you're getting older and your body is starting to change— yet again. Pimples, period woes, weight gain, hair sprouting up in unexpected places—weren't these physical annoyances supposed to be part of your ancient history, along with multicolored slouch socks, scrunchies, and bad home perms? In addition to experiencing physical changes that you previously thought were only associated with adolescence, you'll have some old-lady moments even though you're far from becoming an old lady. (Plus, need we remind you that old ladies can be pretty cool—check out "Twenty-one Old-Lady Things That Are Actually Pretty Cool" on page 162.) For instance, it took you four days (and a bottle of Pepto) to recover from your BFF's bachelorette party, you finally gave in and got a pair of glasses so that you can see the street signs when you drive at night, and, yes, that's a spider vein on your leg. (Sure, it bites, but it won't kill you.)

The New Coming of Age Moments: Health Edition

There's no doubt that your journey to womanhood was tough the first time around when you were up against braces, mosquito bite boobs, and curious feminine hygiene products. Well, guess what? Time for some more fun, only now, you don't have to contend with zits. Actually, never mind. . . .

Puberty	Redo-berty
You beg your mom to let you shave your legs like all the other girls.	Your boyfriend begs you to shave your legs so you look like a girl again.
Stuffing your training bra	Stuffing your ass into a pair of Spanx
Dyeing your hair hot pink with Manic Panic	Panicking when you find your first gray hair
Wondering how much longer you'll have to wait for pubic hair	Wondering how much longer you can go without getting waxed
Worrying that a tampon could get lost "up in there" forever	Discovering that you could have a tampon "up in there" for days before you remember to take it out
Peeing on a pregnancy test stick (and praying that you're not a Lifetime movie in the making)	Peeing on an ovulation predictor test stick (and praying that you're, um, making eggs)
Getting a giant zit on your chin the night before the Spring Fling dance	Getting a giant zit on your chin the night before the spring sales conference
Sneaking ciggies behind the bleachers during gym class with your friends	Rocking the nicotine patch
Learning how to put a condom on a banana during sex ed class	Learning how to put a condom on with your mouth during a fellatio workshop at your friend's bachelorette party (So "super fun," right?!)
Buying a pair of booty shorts to show off your cute little booty	Buying a pair of Bermuda shorts to cover up the not-so-cute cellulite on your butt
Trying to do a middle split during cheerleading tryouts and pulling a muscle	Trying to do "the Bridge" in yoga class and pulling a muscle

Now, let's put things in perspective. You're hardly ready for Shady Acres (although we have to admit that shuffleboard looks pretty fun)—actually, quite the opposite, because you're in the prime of your life, a place where you'll be hotter and more confident than ever. All of this just means that it's time to take greater responsibility for your health—physical, mental, and sexual—if you haven't already. But before we turn into Ms. Dumont, your seventh-grade gym teacher with the modified mullet who wore nylon tracksuits that made a swishy sound when she walked and who doubled as the sex ed teacher (you weren't so lucky to have the school nurse as a teacher of the birds and bees), let's take a look at your current attitude toward your health.

Some Likely Scenarios: Where You're at with Health and Fitness

THE DIET FAD FREAK: From juice fasts and colonics to those As Seen on TV™ foot detox pads and diet pills that have some majorly unpleasant side effects (we still don't quite understand how the words "oily" and "stool" didn't stop you), you never met a health McFix you didn't love for a minute and then abandon for something newer, more extreme, and, most likely, grosser. The Atkins diet? Been there, done that—at least, you did it until you fell off the wagon and right into the endless bowl of pasta at the Olive Garden. The Ab Slide? You ordered one—and now it's conveniently stashed away somewhere in the recesses of your basement (or is it underneath your bed?), along with a ThighMaster, the Billy Blanks Tae Bo DVD set, and a pair of those flip-flops that supposedly tone your ass. Hell, if the iPhone had a Lunchtime Lipo application, you'd be the first person to download it.

Instead of focusing on long-term goals and improving your overall health, you obsess about dropping pounds fast without having to feel the burn (and we're not talking about the burn you experienced in a very, um, uncomfortable place after taking down a whole bag of Baked Cheetos in one sitting). Why let something like rational thinking or basic science stop you when you can eat only cabbage for a week and drop enough water weight to squeeze into those skinny jeans that will bring all the boys to the yard?

Your philosophy in life is best summed up with these four words: "If I could only . . ." It's simple enough, right? If you could only lose ten/twenty/thirty/whatever number of pounds, or fit into your skinny jeans, or take the thunder out of your thighs, or look like a Victoria's Secret angel, then you'd be happy. But, here's the thing: Moving your body and eating right will not only make you look better but make you feel better and live longer, too. Here's another thing: Nobody's perfect, so stop killing yourself to compete with the Photoshopped fantasy images that clutter magazines or the intern at your office who has no visible cellulite as she rocks inappropriately short skirts. (Besides, don't you know that genetics plays a big role in who gets the lumpy stuff?) And, at the risk of getting all Oprah on your ass, you can only be truly happy if you learn to be happy with yourself—or have as much money as the divine Ms. Winfrey does.

STILL PARTYING LIKE IT'S 1999: Let's get this straight: You're not a smoker because you only puff on Parliaments when you're drinking. You're not a drinker because, unlike those tragic people from *Intervention* who can't leave the house without downing a fifth of vodka and a bottle of Robitussin, you only drink when you go out. And you only go out . . . on days that end in "y."

That's right, party girl. Even though you graduated from college years ago, you still hold the sloppy undergraduate lifestyle near and dear to your heart, regularly partaking in Fourth Meal at Taco Bell (the calories don't count if you're drunk), pounding Long Island iced teas with the reckless abandon of a sorority sister who just scored her first fake ID, soaking up UV rays until your skin is as crisp as a BBQed hotdog (you can't help it if you're melatonin-challenged), and getting your exercise by surfing the channels as you camp out on the couch all day.

Sure, living for the thrill of tonight and ignoring tomorrow's inevitable hangover can be great fun—for a bit. But unless you share Keith Richards's mutant, revelry-resistant genetics, all of your imbibing and indulging is going to come back to bite you in the bum, if it hasn't already. Hell, it catches up with the best of us. We're not saying that a girl (sorry, *woman*) can't occasionally have a little fun, but you need to put down the G&Ts and treat yourself with a little TLC. And while you're at it, ditch the pink velour sweat suit.

SUFFERING FROM SUPER-UBER-BUSY SYNDROME: Forget the vintage pop psychology standby *I'm OK, You're OK.* Today, it's more like *I'm Busy, You're Busy.* As you juggle long hours at work and try to maintain some semblance of a personal life, the mere thought of eating a balanced diet, squeezing in workouts, and catching the coveted eight hours of shut-eye each night can seem overwhelming. Heck, sometimes it's hard enough to escape to the ladies' room for a quick pee-pee.

You're suffering from Super-Uber-Busy Syndrome, a modern-day pandemic that results in cutting corners, taking shortcuts, and opting for instant, convenient, drive-thru everything as you struggle to cross off the items on your to-do list. (Number 10: Read that book on time management.) This express-checkout way of life might seem efficient, but you often forget to do your most important task: yourself. Actually, that sounds really dirty (speaking of "She Bop" . . .), so let's rephrase: Multitasking be damned. You need to take care of yourself because taking care of yourself will give you the energy to tackle your busy life. And before you complain that your planner is too packed to fit in some quality *you* time, try rearranging your priorities. By cutting down on your Facebook-stalk-your-ex time or whittling away at your watching-MTV-shows-that-are-way-too-young-for-you-anyway time, you'll be shocked at how the hours find their way back into your day. (OK, we'll give you a pass if you have kids.)

THE HIGH PRIESTESS OF HEALTH: For you, being healthy is more than a lifestyle choice; it's a religion. (Or, more like a cult.) Other people eat, drink, and maybe hit the gym or go for a run. You "eat clean" to nourish your inner self, hydrate with the latest antioxidant elixirs, and hit up a cardio sculpt class before running to a Bikram yoga class (in your $98 Lululemon pants, of course). You follow a macrobiotic vegan diet (just like Gwyneth!) but have been known to pull the ovo-lacto-vegetarian card when presented with a particularly enticing dessert menu. You treat your migraines with acupuncture, and according to your Facebook profile, you're a fan of Buddhism, Kabbalah, and Enya.

Maybe you have too much time on your hands, or maybe you truly love how the Master Cleanse makes you feel (those feelings are also known as "nausea" and "malnutrition"), but whatever the reason for your ~~obsession~~ devotion to your health and well-being, it's getting kind of annoying. See, it's one thing to lecture your friends on the evils of artificial sweeteners, but do you really need to bring your own agave syrup to brunch? And is it really necessary to send out weekly emails about the evils of conventional cosmetics, paper shopping bags, and plastic water bottles? You might think you're being thoughtful, but really your "thoughtfulness" just makes your friends want to shove an eco-friendly Sigg water bottle up your preachy ass.

What's Really Going on When It Comes to Your Health: A Little Psychological Perspective

A lot of anxiety surrounding personal health and fitness in redo-berty years comes from our internal struggles. Sure, there are some realities that we are going to have to deal with as we get older—slowing metabolisms, decreasing muscle mass, and health problems. However, right now, in our quest for elusive happiness, we put a lot of pressure on ourselves to be in the Best. Shape. Evah.

"When it comes to body image, there is a lot of self-blame," says our go-to psychological expert Dr. Kevin. "Our curse is that we always have to be the best we can be."

At the risk of sounding touchy-feely (ah, fuck it—let's get touchy-feely), cut yourself some slack. For example, if you've entered a new workout plan and the weight isn't coming off right away, shut down that bully inside your head who tells you that you're not good enough, you're not smart enough, and doggone it, people don't like you.

In regard to losing weight or getting into shape, "We think it should be easy, but getting over genetics and habits takes hard work," says Dr. Kevin. He goes on to say we need to forgive ourselves and accept ourselves.

We know, easier said than done, but we'll bet that you forgave some a-hole ex-boyfriends for far greater offenses. ("But baaaabe, it's not cheating if it's in a different area code.")

Adult Education: Experts Answer Your Seven Most Burning Health Questions (That sounds kinda painful, right?)

Yes, you're getting a little a bit older, but here's the good news: You're still about a decade away from getting your first colonoscopy! Going to the doctor is never fun (at least when you were a kid they gave you a lollipop after your tetanus shot). These days, you're lucky if you get a Band-Aid before they practically push your bum off the examination table. To help soften the blow, we've rounded up some super-smart experts to tell you what you should and shouldn't be doing right now to stay healthy and happy for many more years to come. Included are Dr. Jennifer Wider, a women's health expert, radio host, and author of *The New Mom's Survival Guide*; Dr. Fredric Brandt, superstar dermatologist; and Lauren Goldberg, personal trainer at Peak Performance in New York City. But first, can we have your insurance card and co-pay please?

Burning Question #1: Here's a biggie: What should I be doing now to look and feel good later on?

No magical cream that contains yucky ingredients such as baby foreskin or bird poop (we wish we were making that up), no masochistic crash diet favored by bobble-headed celebs, and no amount of virgin blood will give you the gift of eternal youth. (Plus, isn't being an adult a lot more fun?) In order to keep yourself looking and feeling great from now until *Saw XXXIV* is released, Dr. Jennifer Wider recommends the following three things (and there aren't any big surprises here, but we think these bear repeating): First of all, maintain a healthy diet and move your body—that means at least thirty minutes of aerobic exercise, five days a week. (More about developing a fitness routine in Burning Question #2.) Second, stop with the ciggies—and that includes you, members of the "I only smoke when I drink" club. "One of the worst things you can do to your body is smoke cigarettes," says Dr. Wider. "Not only does it cause wrinkles and skin issues, but it lines you up for many diseases down the road." And third, protect yourself before you wreck yourself from the sun.

Dermatologist Dr. Fredric Brandt (the man responsible for preserving some of the most famous faces in the world) also stresses that you should shield the skin you're in with SPF. "The most important thing is to apply sunscreen every day—minimum SPF 30, no matter what." He goes on to say that a teaspoon of sunscreen should be used for the face, and an additional teaspoon should be used for each arm. In addition to shielding yourself from the rays, Dr. Brandt recommends developing and following a skincare regimen, if you haven't started already. "Just like you brush and floss your teeth, take care of your skin every day," he says.

Burning Question #2: Does my metabolism really crash and burn at thirty and if so, what can I do about it?

"Crash and burn? Not exactly. But slow down? Definitely," says Dr. Jennifer Wider. (OK, maybe we were being a little overdramatic with this question.) By the age of thirty, our metabolism begins to take things down a notch, but there are things you can do to give it a boost. Dr. Wider says drinking the recommended eight glasses of water a day is important since dehydration can slow things down. Also, you should get seven to eight hours of sleep a night. And finally, when possible, avoid missing meals. "This may have worked in college, but it's not going to work anymore. Skipping breakfast and other meals during the day can trigger the body to store fat. Not only that, but you're more likely to binge later on because you're starving," says Dr. Wider. She suggests keeping your body's metabolism in an active state by eating smaller, more frequent meals throughout the day. Also, regular aerobic exercise is key. (Are you sensing a pattern here?)

Lauren Goldberg, a personal trainer at Peak Performance in New York City, talks about the challenges of getting fit during the redoberty years. "When you're younger, you take your body for granted. You're not in you real body until you hit your late twenties and thirties," Lauren says. "Even if your actual weight doesn't change, your fat distribution changes, meaning you'll notice the little belly tire even if you're not eating any differently or working out less than you were a few years ago. And you're going to have to work harder to see results."

Lauren goes on to say that this is the age when you determine what your fitness level will be when you get older, so use it as an opportunity to become smarter, healthier, and more fit. The first step is committing to a routine. Make it a priority to do something active five days a week—no excuses. You'll need to sweat and get your heart rate up—not feel like you've just gone for a leisurely stroll down the block.

"You don't get a gold star for the 'but I walk everywhere' excuse. That only works if you're sixty," says Lauren. She suggests switching things up with a variety of workouts to counteract your body's "muscle memory." (Walking, biking, yoga, and Pilates will give you the cardio you need.)

Also, those underwater-roller-rebounding classes might sound like fun, but keeping it real with old-school lunges, squats, push-ups, sit-ups, and a good run does the trick. "It's easy to get fancy and carried away with that sort of stuff, but the basics still work the best," says Lauren. Plus, you'll be a lot less intimidated if you're new to working out and don't have to deal with a machine that looks like a medieval torture device.

For those of you who don't like the gym, Lauren recommends getting a workout buddy and making appointments to do active things together, like morning runs. That way, you'll be there to motivate each other and avoid being seduced by the snooze button on your alarm clock.

Burning Question #3: What routine medical tests and exams should I be getting now?

If you've been blessed with the gift of good health, it's easy to slack off when it comes to routine medical maintenance or to simply tell Dr. Google your symptoms and get Internet-diagnosed with a bunch of scary diseases that you used to die from when you played *The Oregon*

Trail in social studies class. ("Do I have typhoid fever? And why are my oxen dying?") As you get older, though, you have to step up your game when it comes to preventative care, especially since the risk of getting some scary stuff increases with age.

We've already talked about the importance of protecting yourself from the sun, so it's not surprising that you need to watch out for skin cancer. "It's one of the largest health threats facing young women in the United States," says Dr. Wider. It's also the number one cancer in men and women, and melanoma, the deadliest form of the disease, is the most common cancer in women ages twenty-five to twenty-nine You'll need to start getting a yearly skin exam with a dermatologist.

Other recommended medical tests that you need to get to ensure that everything is running smoothly include the following: an annual full checkup, including height, weight, blood pressure, and cholesterol (especially if heart disease runs in your family); a dental exam one to two times every year; a Pap test and pelvic exam by the age of twenty-one or three years after you've become sexually active (many doctors recommend getting these done yearly); STD testing (this is absolutely essential, especially if you've ever had unprotected sex); and a vision exam every two years. Generally, you won't have to get a mammogram until you hit forty, but if you have a history of breast cancer, speak with your doctor about other methods of screening that may need to start earlier.

Also, while on the subject of boobs, Dr. Wider notes that there has been some controversy over self-breast examinations and how much they can help, but many studies have shown that women who take an active role in their own health care can make a large difference in their own health. Self-breast exams should be performed once a month about five to seven days after your period has ended.

Burning Question #4: My period seems to be getting worse (heavier and longer) the older I get. Why do I suddenly feel like I'm thirteen again (and not in a good way)?

Ah, the "monthly curse," the "hunt for Red October," the "crimson tide." Whether it's a mild nuisance or a major health problem, getting your period has never been particularly fun. However, as we approach our redo-berty years, many women might notice changes in their monthly ebb and flow—and not in a good way.

"As we age, our periods don't always stay the same. For some women, menstruation seems heavier and longer as they get older. The reason for this can vary from person to person. Some women have benign (harmless) growths called fibroids, which can bulge into the uterine cavity and cause heavier bleeding," says Dr. Wider. She goes on to say that other women notice this pattern after they have a baby and no cause is found. If you notice a sudden change in your period accompanied by pain, severe cramping, or mid-cycle bleeding, you may want to talk it over with your physician. She or he can help uncover the cause and offer the proper treatment to get Aunt Flo under control.

Burning Question #5: What are the best ways to reduce stress?

Just like it's difficult to avoid Heidi Montag and Spencer Pratt, it's also damn near impossible to eliminate stress from our lives. However, we can reduce the negative affects it has on you. Studies have shown that stress can lead to sleeping disorders, skin changes (such as acne), alcohol abuse, and depression. That's why it's so important to find ways to deal with stress. Here are a few tips from Dr. Wider:

1. **Just breathe:** When we stress out, our bodies go into overdrive. Our heart rate goes up and our breathing rate increases, as well. Deep, rhythmic breathing can have a calming effect on the body;

it tends to slow the heart rate back down and levels off rapid breathing.

2. **Get moving:** Overwhelming evidence suggests that exercise is a great way to relieve stress. Studies suggest that physical activity can help lower stress through brain chemicals.

3. **Get by with a little help from your friends:** Having people in your life that you can trust and rely on can be one of the largest stress relievers out there. Good friends and family members who will be there for you no matter what are priceless.

4. **Dump the negative (whether it's people or issues):** Studies show that people who are prone to pessimism can spread negativity to others. Learn to remove yourself from these situations as often as possible.

Burning Question #6: Why do our hangovers now feel like they last for 3 days?

You're out with friends, celebrating a big promotion at work, a milestone birthday, an impending marriage, or the fact that it's Friday night. Cocktails are flowing, the tunes are blaring, and the next morning (and afternoon and evening) you're hurting. We're talking the type of hurt that renders you completely useless, confined to bed with a bottle of Vitaminwater, a can of Pringles, and an *America's Next Top Model* marathon on your television. Hangovers never exactly felt good, but as you get older, partying like a rock star leaves you feeling like you crawled out from underneath an avalanche of rocks the next day.

You can blame age for ruining your good time. There's medical evidence that for some people, hangovers really do seem to get worse with age. In one study reported in the journal *Alcoholism: Clinical and Experimental Research*, the unpleasant physical symptoms associated with alcohol seemed to affect adults more severely than adolescents. The researchers hypothesized that teenagers have a higher resistance to alcohol, which wanes as we get older. Headaches, lethargy, and the ability to rebound the next day may actually worsen as we get on in years. "So if you feel like you're stuck in bed, unable to rally in the morning following a girls' night out, you're not alone!" says Dr. Wider. Which is one of the many reasons why you should drink in moderation, rather than try to down your body weight in margaritas whenever you go out. (Plus, slurring is never sexy.)

Burning Question #7: What's that annoying ticking sound? Please don't say it's my biological clock. . . .

Something weird happens around your thirtieth birthday. Actually, we've already established that a lot of weird things happen around your thirtieth birthday (give or take a couple of years), hence the point of this book, but perhaps the most unsettling occurrence is the sudden awareness of a biological clock. For some women it's a nagging feeling, almost like another thing to put on our to-do list after learning a foreign language and planning a vacation to Reykjavik, while others experience an inexplicable urge to have a baby, like now. On the other hand, if you're thirty and have zero desire to become a mother in the near future (or ever, for that matter), don't assume that your biological clock is broken or that the whole concept of an internal baby timer is a total farce to begin with.

"With all of the high-tech fertility treatments available, some women question the validity of a biological clock. But the hard, fast truth is that clock is not a fictitious; it is very real and some women end up learning this the hard way," says Dr. Wider, who notes that according to many scientific studies, the average woman's ability to get pregnant begins to slow down as early as thirty and by age thirty-seven, a woman's fertility drops significantly. And don't be fooled by those fortysomething celebs who seem as fertile as your average sixteen-year-old cheerleader. "Despite the latest high-tech, cutting-edge medical procedures, it is extremely rare for a woman older than forty-four to have a baby with her own eggs," says Dr. Wider. "Eggs age as women age, making it harder and harder to become pregnant as time goes by." Unfortunately, right now, technology has not been able to change our biology, so the clock keeps on ticking.

Just to be clear, no one is suggesting that you get knocked up today, especially if you're not in an emotional or financial position to have a baby. We're firm believers that things happen for a reason. You just need to be aware of the time constraints that we have to deal with. Is it fair that a rich seventy-eight-year-old man can sire a child with a perky Playmate, while women don't have time on their side when it comes to fertility? Of course not, but now that you've reached grown-ass adulthood, you should realize that some things just aren't fair. Plus, just like puberty, it's only natural.

The Puberty Workout

Forget burning calories on a stripper pole in a cardio-erotic-hip-hop-conditioning class! You can totally lose weight doing the things you used to do during your adolescence. For easy reference, here is a list of common puberty (ick) activities and the number of calories burned per hour. (FYI, this data has been calculated for a 150-pound person, and www.caloriesperhour.com broke everything down for us.)

1. Attending class: 122 calories
2. Chitchatting on the phone (while reclining): 68 calories per hour (or, in your case, 408 calories for 6 hours)
3. Dancing (unfortunately, no data exists for dancing around your room and singing into your hairbrush): 306 calories

4. Doing your hair: 170 calories (you probably burned this many calories just doing your bangs)

5. Kissing a boy (or your pillow): 68 calories

6. Playing badminton in gym class: 306 calories

7. Playing board games: 102 calories

8. Practicing the cello (your parents forced you to): 136 calories

9. Putting on makeup: 136 calories (but will your mother really let you out of the house looking like that, young lady?)

10. Roller-skating: 476 calories

11. Shopping: 156 calories

12. Sitting and doing your homework: 122 calories

13. Smoking (you rebel, you): 68 calories

14. Watching TV: 68 calories

IN CONCLUSION

Now that we're getting a little bit older, it's time we treat ourselves like we do our good friends: with kindness and a touch of brutal honesty. Here's a shot of both: First, we meant what we said about this being the prime of your life. In fact, let us remind you about that British study we talked about earlier in the book which found that women feel sexiest at age thirty-four. And if you're dangerously close to that number, fear not, since the same study reported that fifty-six percent of the participants said they enjoyed sex more in middle age than when they were younger, so that should give you something to look forward to. Now, onto that friendly frankness: You can no longer get away with old habits like getting the majority of your calories from frozen yogurt, drinking more than three adult beverages a day, and staying up until the wee hours of the morning watching infomercials (big girls *really* need their beauty sleep). In summary, here are some main points you should take away from this chapter:

1. Stop beating yourself up about your body. Instead, try beating up somebody else in a kickboxing class.
2. The Internets are not a substitute for a real, live doctor.
3. Sunscreen is your friend.
4. It's time to start treating your body with some TLC.
5. After a night of excess, you might find yourself asking, Is it me, or are my hangovers getting worse as I get older? The answer is this: Age might have a little to do with it, but it's more likely the fact that you drank six margaritas at Señor Swanky's. Remember the old rhyme: Beer before liquor, never been sicker; six margaritas . . . and you wonder why you're hugging the toilet the morning after? Seriously? (OK, so we never said that we were poets.)

Sex Talk: What's Going on Between the Sheets During Your So-Called Life

We know you have sex on the brain, so let's get on with talking about gettin' it on. Below, we put burning questions about your sex life in good hands. Debby Herbenick, Ph.D., MPH, is the associate director of the Center for Sexual Health Promotion; a sexual health educator at the Kinsey Institute for Research in Sex, Gender, and Reproduction, Indiana University; and the author of *Because It Feels Good: A Woman's Guide to Sexual Pleasure and Satisfaction.* Read on for her answers.

Burning Question #1: Is it true that your sex drive increases in your thirties? If so, why?

FROM DR. HERBENICK: Actually, a woman's sex drive is influenced by a range of factors—hormones, health (sleep, eating, exercise), stress, as well as feeling desired. It is not necessarily the case that a woman's sex drive will be highest in her thirties, especially if she is stretched thin between children, a partner, housework, and work. That said, women tend to have some sexual advantages in their thirties—unlike when they were younger, women in their thirties more often feel comfortable with masturbation and thus have learned what type of sexual touch feels good to them. Having had more sexual experience may also help them to feel more comfortable expressing their sexual desires to a partner and also more comfortable initiating sex—all of which can greatly enhance a woman's sex life.

Burning Question #2: I've been with my significant other for a long time, and while I love him to death, I have zero desire to have sex with him. What's up with my libido and how can I reignite our sex life?

FROM DR. HERBENICK: Sexual desire can be influenced by lifestyle habits, medical conditions, medication, and relationship factors. Some sex therapists believe that sexual desire declines in steady relationships at least in part because we know so much about each other and thus have so little mystery left. If your health checks out well at your doctor's office, try to add a little mystery or sense of unknown back into your relationship. Try cultivating some of your own interests by taking a class on your own or spending some time each week with your girlfriends and encourage him to do the same. Then when you are together, you may be more excited to see each other—both with and without clothes on. Check out the book *Mating in Captivity* by Esther Perel for more information.

Burning Question #3: I'm almost twenty-eight/thirty/thirty-two years old and I've never had an orgasm. Is there something wrong with me?

FROM DR. HERBENICK: Many women in their twenties, thirties, and beyond have never had an orgasm—and no, that doesn't mean that anything is necessarily wrong with you. Most women have their first orgasms during masturbation and using a vibrator can make it easier to have an orgasm—a basic silver bullet vibrator or another clitoral-focused toy is often a good beginner's touch. If you're aiming to have an orgasm during intercourse, try a position such as the coital alignment technique (CAT) that is a basic adaptation of missionary. He's on top, you're on the bottom, with his shoulders just past yours. This position is one that involves more pelvic grinding than thrusting and is one of the few positions that's been shown to be helpful to women's orgasm. You can learn more details about this and other orgasmic positions in my book *Because It Feels Good: A Woman's Guide to Sexual Pleasure and Satisfaction.*

Burning Question #4: I'm single and totally paranoid that every guy I go out with has an STD. How worried should I actually be?

FROM DR. HERBENICK: It's wise to be concerned about sexually transmissible infections (STIs). Getting to know a man well enough to have a conversation about his history of STI testing (and diagnosis) can help you to feel more comfortable about your sexual choices. If you'd like more peace of mind, suggest that you get tested for STIs together before having sex.

Burning Question #5: Is it me or does every guy try to get out of wearing a condom? Why is this and what should I do?

FROM DR. HERBENICK: No, not all men try to get out of wearing condoms. In fact, some men prefer to have sex with condoms because they enjoy the protection against pregnancy and infection. That said, some condoms can be uncomfortable for men, especially if the condom isn't the right fit for them. Fortunately, condoms come in different sizes—from snugger fit, to standard fit, and all the way to extra-large sizes. Look online for condoms if your local store doesn't carry a size that feels comfortable to him, and insist that you two use protection before having sex. Condoms remain the only device we have to reduce the risk of HIV and other infections such as chlamydia and gonorrhea.

Burning Question #6: I finally met a really great guy but there's one problem: We're kind of lacking in the sexual chemistry department. Is it possible to become more compatible in bed, or does sexual chemistry have to be an innate thing?

FROM DR. HERBENICK: There's no real way to tell—many couples have chemistry right from the start whereas others start as friends or compatible but low-key lovers and then develop enormous passion for each other later on. If you think that this relationship has potential, try to give it a go—just try to not over-commit until you're ready.

Burning Question #7: I know women talk about their "number." I'm in my late twenties and am pretty inexperienced, which makes me feel really insecure and self-conscious around guys. Any suggestions?

FROM DR. HERBENICK: A gynecologist cannot tell whether a woman is a virgin or has had few sexual experiences just by looking at her—and neither can a sexual partner. As there is no one "good" or reliable technique to use when it comes to kissing, hand stimulation, oral sex, or intercourse, it's not the case that practice makes perfect. You don't need to have a certain number of partners or experiences in order to be a good lover. Instead, try to focus on creating a pleasurable experience with the next person you are with. Take the time to learn how they like to be kissed and touched, and take time, too, to figure out what you like best.

Sounding Off

It could be experiencing one of life's "biggies" (marriage, baby, mortgage, a major promotion). Or it could be the way other people treat you. Regardless of how it happens, now is usually the time that most of us start to feel like grown-ups. Here's what our panel of esteemed ladies had to say in response to: **Was there a particular moment in your life when you realized, "Holy shit, I'm officially an adult!"?**

"The day my dad came to me for advice."—*Brooke, 29*

"Not yet. Maybe when I move out of my parents' house."—*Julie, 29*

"When I peed on the stick and it said 'PREGNANT.'"—*Lori, 30*

"At the beginning of the month when I put six to seven envelopes in the mailbox for all my various bills, this is when I realize that I'm a grown-up. Also, I have a Sears card. Who has those? Adults, that's who."—*Danielle, 26*

"The day my son was born. I realized that I have to be responsible for another life and it is no longer all about me!"—*Candice, 31*

"Uhhhh, was that supposed to have happened already?"—*Jen, 26*

"When I bought my house."—*Cheryl, 30*

"I think I realized this when I wanted to stay at home in my pajamas cuddled up in a blanket on the couch and watch a movie rather than go out to the bars and drink myself silly."—*Jill, 27*

"When I was representing a client in a divorce proceeding in Supreme Court and the judge called me 'counselor.'"—*Mary, 30*

"This is the first year where all of my friends are getting married, and this is the first year where people react strongly to my age saying, 'Wow you're *that* old? You don't look *that* old.' As though twenty-eight is even *that* old!"—*Heather, 28*

"I realized I was officially an adult when my parents stopped sending me grocery money."—*Carla, 27*

Seven

You're Taking a Class for Fun?: Extracurricular Activities, Fun, and Entertainment During Your Off-Hours

WILLY WONKA: So much time and so little to do. Wait a minute. Strike that. Reverse it.

—from *Willy Wonka and the Chocolate Factory*

LET THEM EAT PASTE

We all know about the sad state of the economy, the problems with our health care system, and the threat of global warming. However, there's another crisis looming on the horizon, and this one is directly affecting our nation's most innocent citizens. (FYI, we're talking about children, not the Jonas Brothers.) In our attempt to be busy, stay busy, or at the very least look busy, this country is being faced with a severe shortage of adequate playtime. Seriously, have you seen what kids are up to these days? Toddlers need BlackBerrys to keep track of their playdates, pedicures, and Mommy and Me classical French cooking classes, while kindergartners have had all of the fun—along with their nap rugs—pulled out from underneath them. Beloved traditions like story time, eating paste, and sloppily coloring outside of the lines with big, fat Crayola crayons have been swiftly replaced with reading, writing, chaos theory, and quantum physics. When kids who are barely old enough to go poo-poo in the potty can't even maintain a school-life balance, how are we adults supposed to enjoy the fun things in life?

Now, we fully understand that part of being an adult means sacrificing recess to make way for big-girl responsibilities. Also, in the history of human existence, leisure time is a relatively recent phenomenon that was made possible thanks to the Industrial Revolution and the emergence of the middle class (although we're pretty sure that even our ancestors took the occasional break from hunting and gathering to sing, dance, and get jiggy around the campfire). Discussions about the origins of free time aside, however, when you reach the end of the road, you're probably not going to call out to the nurse and request the presence of your iWhatever-communication-gadget-they-come-up-with-next for comfort. In order to really live life, you have to have one—outside of work.

The thing is, the whole getting-a-life thing is easier said than done, especially during the redo-berty years, long after the era of your mom being in charge of your extracurricular activities. When you were younger and part of the formal education system, hobbies and interests came easily. Shocking as this sounds now, you learned for the sake of learning (or because your parents threatened to ground you if you didn't practice your piano scales). No one was expecting your pom-pom prowess, mad-cool rendition of "Greensleeves" on the clarinet, or mastery of twenty-sided Dungeons & Dragons die to pay for your college education.

The New Coming of Age Moments: Playtime Edition

Whether you were a superstar mathlete or a superstar athlete back then, there are more similarities between your old hobbies and new distractions that you think. Take a look.

Puberty	Redo-berty
Getting mocked for joining the astronomy club	Getting mocked for being a member of the Facebook group "When I Was Your Age Pluto Was a Planet"
Kicking Russia's ass during Model UN	Ogling Anderson Cooper's ass on CNN
Spraining your thumbs after playing Sega Genesis for ten hours straight	Developing a crippling case of "BlackBerry Thumb" after playing *Brick Breaker* on your PDA
Secretly hoping to be the next Danielle Steel as you scrawl juicy tales of eighth-grade intrigue in your diary	Not-so-secretly hoping to get a big fat book deal as you scrawl juicy tales of sex and the single girl in your blog
Saving up your pennies for a denim Calvin Klein skirt	Feeling really old when you find that same exact skirt in your hip local vintage shop
Receiving critical acclaim for your expertly choreographed routine to C+C Music Factory's epic hit "Gonna Make You Sweat" at the spring recital for Miss Debbie's Dance Studio (and by critical acclaim, we mean that your mom gave you a standing ovation, even though you slipped and fell on your fluorescent-spandexed ass while attempting to do a roundoff)	Receiving a lot of uncomfortable stares when you're spotted "freak dancing" with the bride's seventeen-year-old cousin on the dance floor (hey, he told you that he was a senior—in college)
Freaking out when your "Cindy Lopper" Garbage Pail Kid card went missing	Finding out two decades later that your sister traded it on the playground for a neon slap bracelet

Puberty	Redo-berty
Trying not to fall asleep in Hebrew school/CCD classes	Becoming a believer during your first Bikram yoga class
Signing up for Intro to Psychology at the local community college to get AP credit	Signing up for Creative Writing 101 at the local community college—for fun
Trading Baby-Sitters Club books with your friends	Starting a book club with your friends (which is really just an excuse to drink wine and eat an entire wheel of brie)
Tutoring inner-city youth because you want to give back to your community . . . and because it looks good on your college applications	Volunteering for Meals on Wheels because you want to give back to your community . . . and because it looks good on your online dating profile (you're a regular Mother Teresa)

As we get older and throw ourselves into work, relationships, and family, the thought of doing anything that's not on our to-do list seems impossible, sometimes even selfish. Besides, who has time for hobbies when there are bills to pay and errands to run?

Well, recent research shows that most of us do, in fact, have the time. It's just a matter of rearranging our priorities. (As an aside, if you've recently birthed a child, you get a pass for this one.) Get this: According to the Nielsen Company, the average American spends more than 151 hours per month in front of the boob tube, which comes out to be about 4.9 hours per day. (Now, we love us some *Project Runway* marathons, but *damn*. That's a lot of time spent spooning with the remote control.) Even more mind-boggling, according to the U.S. Bureau of Labor Statistics, employed people work an average of 7.6 hours a day, so it's safe to say that we also watch TV like it's our job. Think of all the other fun stuff you could be doing instead of gawking at D-list celebrities as they make desperate plays for relevancy. (Speaking of fun stuff, according to what we're dubbing the Google Institute of Dubious Facts, between the ages of twenty and seventy, the average person spends six hundred hours having sex, which, if you crunch the numbers, ends up being about nine minutes a day. No word if the average person is watching TV during those nine minutes.)

Now, we'll close out our own little version of *Freakonomics* with some science to further our argument that we need to reclaim our hobbies and free time. Recently, researchers at the Mayo Clinic found that exercising your mind in middle age and later in life by doing activities such as reading books (boo-ya!), playing games, crafting, and socializing can help decrease your risk of developing mild cognitive impairment by as much as 50 percent. While not much research has been spent on the benefits of leisure time and hobbies for twenty- and thirtysomethings, we don't need a doctor to tell us that doing something you love reduces stress and can be a hell of a good time. Read on for a look at how you might be handling your free time during your redo-berty years.

The Scenarios: Where You're at with Your Playtime

WORKING GIRL: You work hard for your money, so hard for your money . . . actually, that's about all you do. As the beep, beep, beep of your alarm clock goes off each morning, you feel like you're stuck in one of those Sandra Bullock movies where she plays an uptight workaholic who's in desperate need of a good . . . well, you know what. (Oh you don't know? The answer is *bang.*) You BlackBerry your way through your weekends, haven't taken a vacation since Bush was president (and we're talking Bush the Elder, since you used to own and operate a very lucrative lemonade stand), and cancel on your friends at the last minute because—shocker—something came up at work. So what's the deal? Does your company give out some kind of platinum, diamond-encrusted plaque to the person who works the most? Because unless you're investing every cent you have into your own business, writing a book (cough, cough), or toiling away at the most demanding job in the world (Courtney Love's publicist), we can't help but wonder why you're spending so much time at the daily grind when you could be out there doing so many other fun things like, oh, we don't know, maybe having a life. Not to play therapist, but perhaps you're trying to escape an unpleasant home environment (like a roommate who constantly sings along to show tunes). Or maybe you're using work to fill a void in the relationship department (no offense to your vibrator). Listen, working girl, it's time that you cut to the part of the movie where you joyfully toss your PDA into the nearest body of water and then run off with the smug yet totally irresistible charmer who taught you how to live and love again. Or, at the very least—take a vacation!

ATHLETICALLY UNINCLINED: The mere thought of joining the office softball team gives you Nam-like flashbacks to atrocities committed during middle school phys ed class, like that one time in seventh grade when you nearly lost an eye after "Mean" Jeanine Grabowski, playground bully and proud owner of a Y chromosome, spiked a shuttlecock into your cornea during an intense game of badminton. (By the way, you're ignoring her Facebook friend request because you still fear her after all these years, despite the fact that she's posing in her profile photo with two-year-old twin daughters, a geeky husband, and a chocolate Labrador retriever named Snickers.

And they're all wearing Christmas sweaters—the dog included.)

OK, so you're not a sporty type of gal. Your idea of a triathlon includes walking, chewing gum, and talking on your cell phone at the same time, and you think the Cincinnati Reds make an excellent merlot. But—insert big sigh here—all of your friends seem to enjoy activities where balls fly at their faces (sluts!), and you probably feel a little left out. Well, luckily this is one of those times when it's actually nice to be a grown-up, since unlike back in high school when your lack of athleticism would've relegated you to the role of Gatorade girl or, worse, team mascot, you can pursue a ~~dorkier~~ more intellectual hobby without risking social suicide. For ideas, read the rest of the chapter.

HOLLY HOBBY: Your outside interests include (but are not limited to) scrapbooking, volunteering, baking cupcakes, taking French lessons, salsa dancing, photography, Tai Chi, and gardening. You also head up a pug rescue, play in an adult soccer league, and run marathons for fun. Sure, having a wide variety of interests is a good thing, but either you're embarking on an extremely delayed attempt to get into an Ivy League school, or you're suffering from a severe case of extracurricular ADHD. Symptoms include flitting from activity to activity, possessing a closet full of barely used sporting equipment (seriously, when was the last time you went boogie boarding?), and not having a free weekend until 2013.

We understand that variety is the spice of life, but there's a difference between trying new things and trying absolutely everything. A hobby (or, in your case, *hobbies*) is supposed to help you relax, but when you're juggling too many obligations, it can actually make you more stressed out. If you're finding that you're getting exhausted from all the prescheduled fun or you contemplate starting a doll collection a la Candy Spelling, you might have a problem. The solution?

It's time to cut back on all the *doing* and spend some time just *being*. (Heavy stuff, right?)

MATERIAL GIRL: Back in the nineties, everyone with ovaries (and some heterosexually challenged men) wanted to be just like Cher Horowitz, who spent the majority of her time shopping for clothes made by, like, totally important designers. Hey, we all love a little retail therapy, but when buying stuff is your only hobby (sorry, "brunch" and *Us Weekly* don't count), it makes you seem about as deep as a Frisbee. For a cheaper and more satisfying way to fill your free time and keep boredom at bay, try learning a new skill like knitting, or how about investing? Your bank account will thank you for it. And if you really can't get control of your binge shopping, either apply to become one of Rachel Zoe's minions (love her) or, at the very least, contact MTV since we're sure they'd love to do a follow-up to *True Life: I'm a Compulsive Shopper.*

What's Really Going on When It Comes to Your Free Time: A Little Psychological Perspective

Extracurricular activities might literally be all fun and games, but grown-up playtime offers serious benefits to our mental health. According to our resident psychologist, Dr. Kevin Brennan, having outside interests is important because it gives us different identity positions, and the more identity positions we have, the healthier we are. "The more hats you wear, the better," says Dr. Kevin. This way, you'll be more prepared if and when the going gets tough. For example, getting laid off is never fun, but if you have a life beyond the confines of your cubicle, you won't lose your entire identity along with that regular paycheck, full benefits, and ergonomic office chair. (After all, you're still a great cook and the eighth-ranked fencer in the tristate area, goshdarnit, and no human resources skank can take that away from you.)

Adult Education: Experts Answer Your Five Most Burning Questions about Extracurricular Activities

If you're feeling paralyzed by indecision (should you take up archery, running, or composting? so many choices!), listless from the stresses of your job and your life responsibilities, or underwhelmed by options for fun where you live (you'd rather not hang out in the parking lot of the local 7-Eleven with the high school kids), read on for more advice about getting a life outside of the cubicle. Looking for pointers, we talked to Tina Barseghian, author of *Get a Hobby!*; Anne Fritz, who, along with Hope Schmid, founded the blog *The Jet Set Girls*; and Andrea Murphy, community manager for Meetup.com.

Burning Question #1: I need a hobby. Any advice about developing new interests?

It's time to hit the OFF button on the remote control, tear yourself away from the riveting debate about who wore it best at the Teen Choice Awards (hint: it's probably Hayden Pantyhairs, or however you pronounce her name), and listen up: "If you haven't already developed any interests outside of work, socializing, and reality TV, it's time to take stock. Make a list of your interests and think about what you're already inclined to," says Tina Barseghian. "If you love hanging out at parks and always have fresh flowers in your house, exercise your green thumb and plant your own garden."

Part of the beauty of hobbies is that they don't need to have anything to do with work. (Otherwise, people would unwind on pleasant Saturday afternoons by dabbling in data entry or pharmaceutical sales.) Jet Set Girl Anne Fritz agrees that you should step outside of your comfort zone when trying to find a new interest to pursue in your free time: "Try something totally different from your day job." Anne, who worked as a staff writer at a magazine, made like Demi Moore in *Ghost* and took a pottery class. "It was so different than what I did during the day, I was able to truly immerse myself in it—and the mud," she says.

You should also give yourself permission to be bad at your hobby, which will up the enjoyment factor. "In my pottery class, I realized I was never going to make a living as a master pottery thrower," Anne explains. "I just did if for the sheer joy of getting my hands dirty. I have some pretty clunky bowls I still show off proudly."

Remember, you're living your life, not accumulating activities like a ruthless type-A high school student. Have fun. Get messy. Fail at something and live to tell the tale.

Burning Question #2: I've been experiencing weekend ennui lately. What are some interesting/fun things I can do during the day other than going shopping, seeing a movie, or hitting up brunch?

On the scale of problems, Glamorized Urban Dweller Syndrome (a disorder characterized by overexcessive shopping, brunching, and inability to go anywhere without a venti Starbucks cup in hand) falls somewhere between being too beautiful to get a date and having a hangnail. Still, no one wants to be stuck in a rut.

We asked Andrea Murphy, community manager for Meetup.com (which, by the way, is a fun way to meet new people) for advice. "Social groups are great for test-driving new interests, without the drama of not having an 'opening' to get the conversation started," says Andrea. "When you share a common ground, interest, or desire to learn something new, you have instant rapport with other people."

Trying out activities through an organized group is also neat way to meet friends who are all different ages, which is what life is about (please, this isn't college anymore), especially when spending Friday and Saturday nights at a local club or watering hole has lost its luster (and it will, if it hasn't already). "Unfortunately you don't have much control over a bar scene. It is what it is," says Andrea. "Bear in mind that not everyone your age may share the same hobbies as you. As you develop new interests, you may actually broaden your social circle to include older and younger folks too. Gasp!"

Imagine that.

Burning Question #3: Did I forget to mention that I don't have any money? How do I fill up my free time with stuff that's costs nothing or next-to-nothing?

To quote poet and songstress Jennifer Lopez, love don't cost a thing. And—surprise, surprise—having fun doesn't have to cost very much either. According to Tina Barseghian, you can find out about wallet-friendly events a number of different ways. Your local coffee shop probably has a bulletin board covered with announcements for live music and neighborhood events, and most local newspapers also include listings of free local events, along with things like gallery openings, theater and dance festivals, and concerts. Also, check your local Craigslist under the "ticket" category—people always sell extra tickets to shows and events at deep discounts and sometimes give them away for free. Hobby groups often invite newbies to meetings, where they can socialize and learn more about that particular pastime.

Every city has a reliable local weekly paper with a comprehensive listing of things to do: museum shows, readings, and art fairs. And, if you live in a larger metropolitan area, sign up for the weekly event email newsletters like *Flavorpill* and *DailyCandy*. They'll clue you in to events that have flown under your radar.

Burning Question #4: I'm all right on the hobby front, but I need to take little break from my busy life and go on a vacation. Here's the thing: My friends and I aren't compatible travelers. How do I find normal people to accompany me on my journey?

You don't really know a friend until you jet off to a faraway land together, in search of adventure, only to discover that she's afraid to eat anywhere but McDonald's (she loves the Royale with Cheese) and cries on the phone to her mother every night at the shared phone in the hostel because she's homesick. At twenty-nine years of age. (True story.)

Anyway, if you're truly not compatible as travelers with your close friends, start planning your dream trip and then advertise it to everyone—coworkers, friends of friends, Facebook acquaintances—says Anne Fritz of *The Jet Set Girls*. You're bound to find someone who shares your passion for clubbing in Miami or checking out the latest Chagall exhibit in San Francisco. "This has worked out well for me a few times—once when I wanted to go to Paris for a quick shopping trip. I couldn't rally any of my close girlfriends for a three-nighter across the pond," says Anne. "I mentioned that I was looking for a travel companion to everyone I talked to. A friend of a friend I met at a dinner party signed on, and we had a blast shopping in Galeries Lafayette, along St. Germain and along the Marais."

One word of caution, though: Make sure when you're traveling with someone you don't know well that your expectations for the trip are clearly defined. It helps if you have a location and general idea in mind as to what type of trip you're taking (sightseeing, shopping, lying out by the beach, all of the above). Address your budget, adventure level, and ability to do things on your own ahead of time.

Another option is to take your trip as one singular sensation. You can either join a tour group and meet new friends or go it totally on your own. And don't worry about becoming a *Dateline* special; traveling alone is perfectly safe, as long as you're smart about it.

"If it's your first solo trip, stick with a destination that's easy. That means going somewhere where you speak the language. Research the destination ahead of time to find out how easy it is to get around town, especially in the evening," says Anne.

When traveling alone, your choice of hotel is extra important, too. You don't want to stay at honeymoon central, surrounded by couples playing games of grab ass in public. (For the record, "playing games of grab ass" were our words, not Anne's. She offered up the much nicer "staring lovingly in each other's eyes.") Opt for a trendy hotel in a central location that has a cool bar and restaurant. That way, you can have an evening on the town without ever having to leave the comfort of your temporary digs.

Burning Question #5: I want to give back. How can I find a great cause to support?

We're so glad you asked. To put it simply, doing good makes you feel good. Helping out people who are less fortunate than you and volunteering for worthy causes help put the trials and tribulations of life in perspective. Once you lend a helping hand, you take the focus off ME, ME, ME and often end up realizing that your problems are, in fact, "problems" (with an emphasis on the quotes). It's safe to say that being selfless gives you the ultimate high—that, and it'll make you seem like a really good person, which, let's be honest, is the *real* reason you want to "give back." (Just kidding.)

If you're overwhelmed by the sheer number of charities out there and don't know where to start, think small for big results. (You don't need to go all Angelina Jolie, traveling the far reaches of the globe, to make a difference.) "Find something close to you, because charity truly begins at home," suggests Andrea Murphy. "Think of how many problems you could easily solve in your own hometown if you put your mind to it." Andrea goes on to mention some volunteer work. "My favorite example of this is the Random Acts of Kindness Meetup. They've totally redefined how I view charitable work. They're making sandwiches for the homeless, holding fund-raisers for worldwide causes, sending care packages to soldiers, building houses, taking the time to visit senior centers, expanding recycling programs, and creating community gardens."

There are plenty of Web resources out there that help match eager volunteers to a great cause. Idealist.org lets you search for local and national organizations and even job listings. Charity Navigator (www.charitynavigator.org) is also a great resource that rates charities and provides information about their financials.

Something else to consider: combining an interest with charity work. This will allow you to pursue your passion *and* do some good. "If you're curious about gardening, sign up as a volunteer with the local park. If you're into set design, call your local nonprofit theater company," adds Anne Fritz.

Find a Great Hobby by Watching Television

Still paralyzed by fear at the thought of leaving your television "stories" behind as you pursue fun stuff out there in the big bad world? Fear not. Let the boob tube guide you to finding a new passion in life.

If you watch . . .	Then you should try . . .
The Hills/The City/any other "reality" show featuring overprivileged, big-sunglass-wearing beach babes and the "bros" with whom they love shopping, texting, and pushing around food on their plates but not actually eating anything	Community theater (you're drawn to stellar acting)
The History Channel	Doing Civil War reenactments

If you watch . . .	Then you should try . . .
Weeds	Urban, um, gardening—yeah, that's it: grow an herb garden
Daytime talk shows and soaps: Dr. Phil, Maury, All My Children, All Dr. Phil's Children . . . yeah, these shows run together in our minds	Sending out job résumés
Lost	Hiking
Animal Planet	Fostering incontinent bulldogs
Grey's Anatomy/House/other hospital dramas	Candy striper
Golden Girls reruns	Knitting and scrapbooking
A Shot at Love with the Jersey Shore/Paris Hilton/whomever	Repeatedly banging your head against a wall

IN CONCLUSION

It's time that we take our free time seriously. No, seriously. (See, we're already starting.) Hobbies, extracurricular activities, and vacations help balance our lives, put pesky things like work in perspective, and give us a better sense of self. Plus, it gives us a chance to have a little fun. Now, here's what you should take away from this chapter:

1. When it comes to hobbies, try something that's totally different from your day job, and don't be afraid of failure.
2. The average American watches a buttload of TV. To refresh your memory, by "buttload," we mean 155 hours per month. In other words, get your butt off of the couch and do something.
3. Give volunteering a try. You might like it!
4. Studies have shown that activities such as reading, crafting, and socializing might help keep you from losing your damn mind when you get older.
5. Contrary to what The Hills tells you, "shopping" is not a hobby.

Twenty-one Old-Lady Things That Are Actually Pretty Cool

Who says that kids get to have all the fun? Here's a list of things your aunt Rose probably enjoys that, frankly, are pretty effing awesome.

1. Knitting
2. Food in jars (OK, *certain* foods in jars. Pickles get two thumbs up, but pickled herring, not so much.)
3. *Antiques Roadshow* (or is that more of an old-gay-man thing?)
4. Reading glasses
5. Mahjong
6. Gel-filled shoe inserts
7. Napping
8. BINGO!
9. Silver hair
10. Banana bread
11. Half slips
12. Crossword puzzles
13. Gardening
14. Tea
15. Sitting on the porch
16. Watching "stories"
17. Witch hazel (it smells like dirty ass, but it can zap zits)
18. Drinking Manhattans

19. Black-and-white portraits (the original Glamour Shots—well, either that, or all grandmas used to look like movie stars when they were younger)
20. Joan Rivers
21. Being so old that you don't give a flying fuck about what other people think anymore

Parents Are People, Too: Family Matters

> HOPE STEADMAN: I think that our parents got together in 1946 and said, "Let's all have lots of kids, and give them everything that they want so they can grow up, and be totally messed up and unable to cope with real life."
>
> —from the pilot of *thirtysomething*

CHILDHOOD'S END

If it hasn't happened yet, it will. Just wait. One day, while you're talking to your mother on the phone, she'll interrupt your regularly scheduled topics of conversation (i.e., who's having a baby, who got fat, and who got fat after having a baby) with something along the lines of, "So, your father and I have been thinking about doing a little redecorating. . . ." Then, she'll launch into a monologue about gray versus taupe and the benefits of track lighting, while you'll interject a steady stream of "uh-huhs" and "oh reallys" to make it seem like you're actually listening.

It's not until the next time you visit your parents' place (which you still refer to as "home," even though you haven't lived there in, like, a decade) that you'll discover the startling truth: "A little redecorating" actually meant "destroying the sanctity of your youth." That's right, faster than you can say "childhood's end," your parents transformed your old bedroom into the wall-to-wall carpeted home office of their dreams (complete with a StairMaster-turned–laundry rack). Gone are your tapestries, high school yearbooks, and love letters, relegated to a big brown box in the attic, along with Mr. Bojangles, who was more than a Pound Puppy—he was a friend.

You feel conflicted about the transformation of the space that served as a haven from the drama of your 'tween- and teenage-wasteland years. The adult in you knows that it's your parents' home, and if they want to sponge-paint the walls a vomitous shade of orange (sorry, "Soft Pumpkin") or fill the backyard with those creepy garden sculptures from the SkyMall catalog, then so be it. Plus, let's get real here. The freedom to redecorate their own property as they please is a small reward for raising you, which couldn't have been easy, especially during your hippie womyn phase in late high school, when you stopped wearing deodorant and shaving your pits in order to subvert patriarchal notions of femininity.

There's another part of you, though, the melodramatic adolescent, who tries to rear her pimply face during times like these. Upon discovering that your beanbag chair has been replaced by ergonomic office furniture, she wants to shout, "Stay out of my room!", slam the door, crank up the volume on her boom box, and collapse into a sobbing heap on her Laura Ashley bedding (because nothing says "rage against the machine" like a rose-patterned dust ruffle).

This bipolar behavior—finally recognizing that parents are people, too, but also fighting off the urge to pout and stomp your feet at the first sign of familial conflict—comes with the territory once you hit the redo-berty years. On one hand, you get older and realize that you have more in common with your parents than you previously thought (besides an addiction to *Dancing with the Stars*—and don't deny it, because we know you can't get enough of "celebrities" donning spandex and doing the samba). You grow to understand that Mom and Dad are also Bob and Susan, who—shockingly—have lives that don't completely revolve around you. (And, thanks to their new home office, Bob reads huffingtonpost.com and Susan dabbles in online social networking.) On the other hand, old habits and family dynamics are tough to break, which is why you still whine like a little bi-yatch when your sister changes the channel because, hey, you were, like, totally watching that episode of *Project Runway* that you've already seen five times before.

Here's the thing about family as you get up there in years: No matter how many candles you blow out on your birthday cake or how many friends your mom acquires on Facebook (actually, she calls it "FaceSpace"), there will always be moments when you want to revert to familiar roles, be it daughter or sister, the baby of the brood or the only child, the caretaker or the taken-care-of. Part of being an adult, though, is acting like one, even during those frustrating times your family still sees you as that gangly girl who sported a mouth full of braces encircled with fluorescent-colored mini–rubber bands (remember those awful things?). That being said, you better watch your tone, young lady!

The New Coming of Age Moments: Family Edition

While you've come a long way from walking ten feet behind your mother at the mall because you were afraid that someone from school might see you two together, the redo-berty years still bring about some familial tension.

Puberty	Redo-berty
Nearly dying from embarrassment when your dad walks in on you and your boyfriend sucking face instead of studying for your history final	Nearly dying from embarrassment when you walk in on your parents doing it instead of watching *Dateline*

Puberty	Redo-berty
Idolizing cool Aunt Darlene, a free-spirited artist who lets you eat ice cream for dinner and stay up late whenever she baby-sits you	Being the cool aunt to your niece and letting her eat ice cream for dinner and stay up late whenever you baby-sit her
Going to a Rage Against the Machine concert with your friends . . . but having to get a ride with your parents	Going to the American Idols Live! Tour with your mother
Wanting to, like, totally barf, when your friends tell you that your older brother is cute	Wanting to, like, totally barf, when your sorority sister marries your older brother ("Now we can be sisters for real!")
Listening to your parents express concern that you're too young to be getting serious with a boy	Listening to your parents express concern that you're too old to *not* be getting serious with a boy
Squealing in delight as wacky Uncle Lou pulls quarters out of your ears and performs other amusing party tricks	Realizing that Uncle Lou is wacky and fun because he's been drunk for the past thirty years
Posing for cheesy family portraits at the JCPenney photo studio, which will inevitably come back to haunt you in twenty years	Making your own family (including the dog) pose for cheesy family portraits that will inevitably come back to haunt them in twenty years
Asking your dad, "Are we there yet?" every five minutes during your drive to the family lake house	Knowing exactly when you'll get to the family lake house because you have GPS in your car but whining every five minutes anyway
Throwing a party at your house when your parents leave town for the weekend	Throwing a dinner party at your house when your parents visit you for the weekend

Puberty	Redo-berty
Yelling at your sister when she borrows your favorite jeans without asking first	Yelling at your sister when she borrows your favorite jeans without asking first (some things never change)

We also realize that, unlike every character Keanu Reeves has played since *Bill and Ted's Excellent Adventure*, not all families are exactly the same. For instance, maybe Bob and Susan haven't slept in the same bed since you were in high school, and it's not just because Bob snores like an asthmatic pug. Or, in your family, maybe Bob and Susan are actually Bob and Steve, Susan and Cathy, or just Susan. No matter who raised you—mom and dad, a single mother, two dads, or Matthew Fox (let's hear it for *Party of Five*), your redo-berty years will present challenges and force you to actually like an adult around your family. And, to further celebrate diversity, let's look at several familial situations you might be experiencing as you enter your late twenties and early thirties.

Some Possible Scenarios: Where You're at with Your Family Life

STUCK IN DYSFUNCTION JUNCTION: Forget Bob and Susan/Bob and Steve/Susan and Cathy/Susan. Perhaps your relationship with your mom makes Lindsay and Dina Lohan seem downright normal. (Doesn't every mother-daughter duo share a penchant for skintight dresses, vodka Red Bulls, and getting "up in da club"?) Or, even worse, maybe your relationship with your father makes Lindsay and Michael Lohan seem healthy. (Who wouldn't suffer from "exhaustion" and "dehydration" if her dad called up TMZ every time she had a fight with her significant other?)

You used to think that once you reached adulthood, your family's rating on the dysfunction meter would magically drop from *Jerry Springer* crazy to *7th Heaven* tranquil. Then you grew up and realized that just because you have a mortgage doesn't mean that your step-mom is going to give up her three-martini lunches . . . and dinners . . . and breakfasts. OK, so you can't choose your family or beat yourself up over every crazy thing they do, but you can own up to your mistakes and overcome a bad childhood (for more information, see Barrymore, Drew). And it's a crappy consolation prize, but at least you know who's to blame for your bad body image/fear of abandonment/habit of dating men who stepped right out of a Lifetime movie. (Let's get this straight: He's got three kids, two ex-wives, and four years in the federal penitentiary under his belt, and you're wondering why this relationship isn't working out? Hmm . . . beats the hell out of us.)

CH-CH-CH-CHANGES: Thanks to countless corporate motivational posters ("If you're not riding the wave of change, you'll find yourself beneath it"), a line uttered by Ferris Bueller that launched a million high school yearbook quotes ("Life moves pretty fast—if you don't stop and look around once in a while, you could miss it"), and the lyrical genius of eighties girl group Exposé ("Seasons change, people change"), we know this much about life: It happens, and shit happens. While the logical part of your brain understands that drama is inevitable, you always expected the shit to start happening at some arbitrary future date (let's say, when you're forty-five), when you would be fully equipped to deal with turmoil. But here you are right now, awash in a wave of change and sea of shit. Yucky.

Maybe you're grappling with a sick parent or a death in the family, two painful ordeals that even we can't joke about, so we'll move onto something more comical, albeit tragically so. Perhaps your parents blindsided you with the announcement that, after twenty-five years of marriage, things just weren't working out anymore. Then—faster than your mom could utter, "I love your father but we're no longer in love," or your dad could say, "But Michelle's an old soul" (translation: Your future stepmom is only four years older than you are)—you joined the estimated 40 percent of adults ages eighteen to forty who come from a broken home. Even though you've reached grown-up status, you still feel blindsided by this change of events. However, after a quick bout with denial, anger, bargaining, and depression, you finally accept the fact that your parents deserve to be happy. And, in this case, happiness takes the form of your mom getting together with Larry, an accountant she met on eHarmony, and your father becoming a grandpa-dad when Michelle, the natural food chef who captured his heart from the elliptical machine at the YMCA, gives birth to Dakota Rose. (Hey, you always wanted a baby sister.)

SCARED TO CUT THE CORD: Holy Joe and Tina Simpson! Your parents are so hyperinvolved with your life that they put to shame those scary pageant mothers who bleach, spray tan, and shellac their toddlers into mini Real Housewives of Orange County in a sad attempt to relive their own glory days as Queen of the Cow Pie/Cheese Curd/Tractor-Pulling Festival. Your mom stayed up all night making your sixth-grade science project and nearly had a nervous breakdown when her papier-mâché volcano burped up baking soda all over your teacher's shoes. Your dad got ejected from your softball games for his "overly aggressive" coaching tactics, and when it came time to apply to college, he wrote your entrance essays. Your personal favorite? His 1,500-word ode to the woman who influenced you the most: Eleanor Roosevelt.

For every misstep, misfortune, and breakup, your helicopter parents have always flown in and made everything better. So is it really any surprise that they still hover around the adult you, micromanaging, coddling, and boo-boo kissing? While it's nice that your parents care so much, sometimes you can't help but think that they're living your life, not you. Yes, they only want to see you happy, but the next time you find yourself in a pickle, do not take a bailout from Mom and Dad. Instead, do what real grown-ups do: Consult the Internet for questionable advice. Or, in all seriousness, take care of your problems your own damn self.

YOU'RE BAAAA-ACK!: You remember that "wave of change" we talked about earlier—the words of wisdom taken from a Successories poster? Well, that wily wave has pulled you into the sea and spit you out in the most unexpected of places: underneath your parents' roof! That's right—thanks to layoffs, the bad economy, or some other unfortunate turn of events, you've joined the boomerang generation: adults who move back in with Mom and Dad after spending time living on their own. Fear not, because you're hardly alone. As reported in a semi-recent *New York Times* article ("Caught in the Safety Net," by Joyce Wadler, May 13, 2009): "According to the Census Bureau, as of last year there were 5.1 million Americans age 25 to 34 living in the home of a parent—a dramatic increase over the 4.3 million who were doing so in 2004." Even crazier, the article goes on to cite research from AARP, which surveyed 1,000 adults in the spring of 2009 and found that "11 percent of people between ages 35 and 44— traditionally the high-earning years in which adults come into their own professionally—were living with parents or in-laws."

That being said, you feel grateful that your parents have the means to help you through this rough patch, yet slightly irked that you have to play by their rules, which in turn, makes you feel guilty because, well, you feel grateful that your parents have the means to help you through this rough patch. Here's some advice: Do not get too comfortable in la casa de Bob and Susan (although we agree that your mom makes a mean chicken cacciatore) or too annoyed when your father leaves his toenail clippings on the bathroom floor (gross, but it's his house, after all). It's one thing if you've hit a really rough patch and are lucky enough to have parents who can help you get back on your feet, but it's quite another if you actually start embracing life underneath their roof, using their emotional and financial support as a crutch—a way to avoid adult responsibilities. It may sound harsh, but we think that there should be some shame if you feel perfectly content to reside in your childhood bedroom when you're old enough to use anti-aging under-eye cream.

What's Really Going on When It Comes to Your Family: A Little Psychological Perspective

According to Dr. Kevin Brennan, family-related angst during the redo-berty years has a lot to do with our endless pursuit of happiness. (Who would have thought that trying to be happy could make us so miserable?)

"Remember that the generational pressures to 'be happy' come from our parents," Dr. Kevin reminds us. He goes on to say that much of the trouble comes from the difference between what "happy" means to parents versus their kids. "Parents may think that, for example, monetary success means 'happy,' when in fact pastry making means 'happy' to the kid," Dr. Kevin says. "Also common is the opposite—especially if your parents were hippies. They want you to strive for art or personal expression, when you want stability, i.e., a job that pays really well."

At this age, you might also grapple with disappointing Mom and Dad. This begs the question: "How can I disappoint a parent who just wants me to be happy?" The simple answer is this: What if you are not happy? By now you should be happy, right, and by now you should know what you want out of life, right? Your parents didn't put any pressure on you, so why aren't you happy yet? (OK, so maybe that answer wasn't so simple after all.)

"Basically, parents start to get a little fed up with you not being fulfilled already typically around the quarterlife," adds Dr. Kevin.

When asked if relationships with our parents get better with age, Dr. Kevin says that they probably will because, in our usual pursuit for happiness, we all tend to go "find ourselves" through therapy. (Hi, Mom and Dad!) "Any shrink will tell you, topics of therapy have mostly to do with your parents," adds Dr. Kevin. "The more aware we are of our family dynamics, the better we will be at attempting to repair our relationships with Mom and Dad."

But remember, even the idea of going back to repair our relationships with our parents is part of that same privileged rule set that says we should. Our parents didn't try that with their parents. Your grandparents didn't even have it as a thought that you should or could have "better relationships." "What the heck is that?" they would say. (Hi again, Mom and Dad!)

Adult Education: Experts Answer Your Most Burning Questions About Your Family

Thanks to eighties and early nineties television sitcoms, we know that families come in all shapes, sizes, and dysfunctions. Yet even if you grew up in a house where everyone was as loving and well adjusted as the Huxtables, you're bound to have at least a little familial shtick, especially during your redo-berty years when you expect to be treated like an adult despite the fact that you still have Daddy's credit card for "emergencies" (more on that touchy subject later on).

We won't pretend to know how to deal with some of the parental and sibling drama that you're experiencing right now, so we called on some people who do it for a living: Dr. Elaine Garrod, a licensed psychologist; Dr. Jane Isay, author of *Walking on Eggshells: Navigating the Delicate Relationship Between Adult Children and Parents*; and Dr. Jenn Berman, a licensed psychotherapist and author of *The A to Z Guide to Raising Happy Confident Kids*.

And for those of you who have a, shall we say, less than cordial relationship with your parents, we can only assume that you're hard at work on a memoir that will put *Running with Scissors* to shame.

Burning Question #1: Is it weird that I speak to my mom everyday?

Confession: This question actually came from Andrea, who calls her mother at least once a day. Sometimes they have serious discussions about politics or the current state of Jennifer Aniston's love life, but mostly it's the *really* important stuff like whether or not you should buy the sweater in both colors if it's on sale (the answer is always "yes") or the difference between the "bake" and "broil" setting on the oven. None of her friends have come right out and said it, but Andrea suspects they think she's too dependent on her mom. While Andrea calls her mom to ask her what she thinks, here's what the experts had to say on the topic.

What was considered a normal amount of contact between a parent and adult child a decade ago has changed dramatically thanks to the multiple forms of communication we now have today, says Dr. Garrod. "People, including our parents, are always accessible, and as a result we've come to expect an instant connection with them."

Enhanced communication aside, mothers and daughters have been close since the beginning of time, and if you're one of those people who gets along so well with your mom that you want to talk everyday, you shouldn't feel bad about that, says Dr. Isay.

But that doesn't let all the mommy's girls (or daddy's girls, if your father is your go-to parent) out there off the hook entirely. "If you cannot make a decision without your mother's approval first, then there is a problem," says Dr. Berman. She goes onto explain that one of the developmental tasks we're supposed to accomplish during our teens and twenties is to individuate from our parents. "When you accomplish this, you develop trust in your own judgment and instincts and let go of seeking out a parent's approval," she says.

Final word: It's cool to talk to your 'rentals multiple times a day just as long as it's for the right reasons (because you love them) and not the wrong ones (because you don't know how to wipe your own ass).

Burning Question #2: Should I feel lame that I'm still taking money from my parents?

Before we even get into this one, Andrea wants to make it clear that this question did *not* come from her; however, in stating that, she is in no way implying that she's above the occasional "donation." Moving on. . . .

Thanks to our uncertain economy, many people are turning to their parents for financial aid. But even if the Bank of Mom and Dad is open for business, does that make it okay to take the money and run?

"It depends," says Dr. Garrod. "If you're in a city or other environment where things are very expensive to make even the minimum requirement to live, and if you are not bankrupting your parents to help yourself out, then it is okay. But if you are not working at all or going to school and are doing nothing but depending on your parents at age thirty, you should feel lame."

You also need to keep in mind that if you accept money from your parents, it might come with conditions.

"If you feel pressured to follow your parent's advice because they're subsidizing your life, then it might be time to cut the purse strings," cautions Dr. Isay.

Our advice? If you're parents are generous enough to help you out monetarily in adulthood, you better not be using their hard-earned dough for "necessities" like an "It" bag or to-die-for shoes. Unless you're an heir to a hotel/cosmetics/tire/shipping fortune.

Burning Question #3: How can I get my parents/siblings/relatives to stop pressuring me to get married/get a real job/have a baby? It's ironic that the same people who made you wait until you were sixteen to go on a date and forbid your boyfriend to sleep—just sleep—in the same room as you just a few years ago are now practically forcing you to go out with anything with a penis or, if you're in a relationship, begging you to set a date and make them grandparents (preferably in that order, but at this point, they're not being picky). Marriage and babies aren't the only things that parents (and other well-meaning yet extremely annoying relatives) like to nag you about. Your career is also a hot topic around the Thanksgiving table. ("Why can't you be an accountant like your brother?" "What's a 'manager of social media' anyway?")

As Will Smith eloquently put it, "parents just don't understand." No really. "Parents worry because their kids seem to be lagging behind their own timetables," says Dr. Isay. She recommends explaining to them that this is more of a generational thing than a personal thing. You can do this by citing the number of friends you have that have gotten married or decided on a career much later on (perhaps through a nice scatter plot).

Dr. Berman points out that, with the exception of your parents, a lot of time your relatives aren't pestering you about your life because they actually care; they do it because they are making conversation and don't know what else to talk to you about. "It's up to you to set boundaries," she says. How you choose to go about that is up to you. If someone asks you a question that makes you uncomfortable, you can diffuse it with humor ("Why, do you have a husband for me?")

or by letting them know outright that your personal life is off limits ("That's a really sensitive subject"). Dr. Garrod agrees that it's up to you to take control and claim your own life: "People stop pressuring you when you stop letting them."

Burning Question #4: Help! I'm a grown-up and I can't be in the same room with my siblings without getting into an argument.

Be honest. What you're really saying is that you're still mad at your brother for cutting off all of your Cabbage Patch Kid's yarn hair and that you're still holding a grudge against your sister from that one time she dropped you on your tailbone during a game of Light as a Feather, Stiff as a Board. And while your inner child is telling you to retaliate with nasty name-calling and perhaps an ambush of Wet Willies, our experts agree that those old habits need to go the way of throwing temper tantrums and wearing a banana clip in your hair. "Stop regressing," says Dr. Berman. "It's easy to get sucked into old family dynamics, but you should find new, mature ways to communicate with your siblings." If that sounds way too easy for you and you want to analyze your behavior, then consider the possibility that you're acting out because you're still competing with your siblings for your parent's attention, says Dr. Garrod, who goes on to say that waiting to see who will be deemed "the favorite" is a totally pointless pursuit. (Anyway, it's so obviously your sister).

While we're on the topic of how to behave around your family now that you're an adult, we'd be remiss if we didn't acknowledge the holidays. You know, that time of year when even the most mature of us revert to brat status. "It seems to be the law of families that grown kids blow up at their parents and one another within three or four days of being home," says Dr. Isay. Her advice: Make sure you get out of the house for a few hours every day to maintain your cool. Our advice: liquor, and lots of it.

Burning Question #5: My parents are getting older and I'm freaking out about their health. What can I do to control my anxiety? You're in good company. "We all feel anxious about the thought of our parents dying," says Dr. Berman. She recommends making peace with the reality that at some point, everyone is going to die (cheery stuff, we know). One way to accomplish this is by talking to a therapist or a spiritual advisor who can help ease some of our anxiety about death. You should also keep in mind that this fear has a lot to do with worrying about the future, more specifically, your inability to control it, says Dr. Garrod. She teaches her clients to become more mindful and appreciative of the present instead of focusing so much energy on what may or may not happen. Unfortunately, we have no jokes to make here.

What Your Mom Says Versus What She Really Means

Moms, they say the darndest things . . . over and over and over again. Here, we translate the most cryptic maternal expressions to reveal the difference between what she says and what she means.

What Your Mom Says	What She Means
Your face is going to freeze like that.	We should've put your bat mitzvah money toward a nose job.
He seems like a nice boy.	At least you're not a lesbian.
We expect more from you.	But not as much as we expect from your sister.
Just wait until you have kids.	I know, because I did the same thing to my parents.
Why buy the cow when the milk is free?	That's how I got your father to marry me.

What Your Mom Says	What She Means
I love all my children the same.	But we love the dog a little bit more.
I'm not angry, just disappointed.	I'm angry *and* disappointed.
You're not getting any younger.	Neither am I.
I was young once, too.	I tried it once, but I didn't inhale.
I want you to be happy.	I want you to be happy. It's just that my idea of happiness is different than yours.

IN CONCLUSION

The redo-berty years have a tendency to bring on a boatload of new family drama that makes you want to sulk at the dinner table or yell, "I wish I was never born!" and slam your bedroom door. But you're an adult now and it's time to learn how to communicate with your parents and siblings in a mature way (physical combat is out, but a little bit of name-calling is still acceptable). Family—you can't live with them, and you can't live without them. Actually, you're a big girl now, so there's a good chance that you don't have to actually live with them anymore, so let's rephrase. Family—you don't have to live with them, but you still can't live without them. To help you make it through the next family function without any bloodshed, here are five main points you should take away from this chapter:

1. Your parents love you and want to be happy—it's just that your idea of happiness isn't always the same as theirs.
2. You are a grown-up. Resist the urge to regress to petulant adolescence around your family. Even when your bitchy little sister borrows your favorite jeans without telling you.
3. It's OK if you talk to your mother everyday on the phone. Just

make sure that you are capable of wiping your own ass without seeking parental guidance first.

4. Bob and Susan have lives that don't revolve around you. Deal with it.

5. Just wait until you have kids.

Flashback: The Tao of Danny Tanner

They don't make television shows like they used to. During what were most likely your adolescent years (and ours, too), feel-good comedies and riveting teen dramas kept us glued to the small screen, watching each week as our favorite characters navigated family life, got caught up in romantic entanglements, and tried to survive high school. Read on for some of our favorite shows from that time period and what you can learn from them during your grown-ass adult years. (Just a note about our methodology for choosing these shows: It wasn't too scientific. Basically, we stuck to our favorite shows from the our adolescence. Sure, *The Cosby Show* was completely awesome, but we watched it when we were kids in its heyday, before puberty started creeping in. As for the appropriately named *Growing Pains*, we've already made one crack at Kirk Cameron's expense in this book, and we'd like to keep it that way.)

THE SHOW: *Full House*

A BRIEF REFRESHER: Single dad Danny Tanner raises his daughters DJ, Stephanie, and Michelle (played, respectively, by Candace Cameron, Jodie Sweetin—the one who ended up writing a tell-all book about her raging meth addiction—and the Olsen twins, long before they grew up and started modeling for House of Derelicte) in San Francisco with the help of Uncle Jesse and some Canadian guy who dumped Alanis Morissette and drove her to write an angry-girl anthem about going down on him in a theater. The show features the ups and downs of family life, including sibling squabbles, girl trouble, and uber-annoying next-door neighbor Kimmy Gibbler. Later episodes touch upon topics such as drinking and boys, but in the most family-friendly way possible. Remember—this was long before we lost our innocence to *Gossip Girl*. In the Tanner clan, when the going gets tough, patriarch Bob Saget cues the cheesy music, gathers his girls together for a powwow, and serves up a dose of verbal Valium known as a Danny Tanner Moment, which makes everyone forget their cares and feel all warm and fuzzy inside. Kind of like real Valium.

WHAT YOU CAN LEARN FROM THIS SHOW TODAY: Danny Tanner doles out some really good advice, so don't be afraid to turn to your parents if you need some guidance in your life. They've seen some things in their time and—surprise, surprise—have probably been through a lot of things that you're going through. And here's another tidbit of wisdom, courtesy of *Full House*: As you get older, you may find yourself complaining that all the eligible men are gross, fat, and bald. Our response: That's really unfair, not to mention kind of shallow. Plus, have you seen Uncle Jesse lately?! Like fine wine, we say. Like fiiiine wine.

THE SHOW: *Saved by the Bell*

A BRIEF REFRESHER: An unlikely group of friends makes their way through Bayside High before moving on to college at California University, an institute of higher learning that you won't find in a Princeton Review guidebook because it doesn't actually exist. The cast of characters includes charming (and bleached blond) Zack Morris, super-popular Kelly Kapowski, leggy overachiever Jessie Spano, fashionista (and scrunchie aficionado) Lisa Turtle, dweeby Screech, and super jock A.C. Slater. (By the way, in real life, Mario Lopez has some Benjamin Button shit going on.) There's silliness, there's drama, there's hanging out at the Max, and, of course, there's the scene to end all scenes: Elizabeth Berkley's precursor to Julianne Moore's epic meltdown at the pharmacy in *Magnolia*. Overwhelmed by the pressures of studying for a geometry test and singing in her girl group (which, by the way, was called the Hot Sundaes), type-A Jessie gets by with a little help from her friends. In this case, her "friends" are highly addictive and dangerous, um, caffeine pills. After Jessie ditches her group's big performance, Zack Morris eventually finds her passed out in her bedroom. One moment she's as groggy as Paula Abdul, and the next she's babbling like a crackhead in desperate need of a rock and a spoon. Zack offers Jessie a one-man intervention, and she collapses into his arms, admitting that she's so excited, so excited, yet so . . . so scared.

WHAT YOU CAN LEARN FROM THIS SHOW TODAY: The *Saved by the Bell* gang is a mismatched bunch, comprised of people from all different walks of life (dweebs, jocks, cheerleaders, brainiacs, etc.). Yet, despite their differences, they all manage to stay friends, picking each other up when they fell down and kicking back at the Max. In fact, their whole is greater than the sum of their parts. Or something to that effect. Later on in this book, in Intermission #11, "The Tao of Judy Blume," we examine the power of unlikely friendship in the tearjerker of a book *Bridge to Terabithia*. The same rule applies here; you and your pals don't need to be carbon copies of each other. In fact, it pays to have a diverse group of friends. Also, another tidbit of advice from the show that can apply to your grown-up life: Let Jessie Spano's pill-popping-induced meltdown serve as a wakeup call. Even though you're well beyond the years of peer pressure, it can still happen. Today, a group of pushers are just waiting to drive you into a life of drugs. Their aliases? Dunkin' Donuts, Starbucks, and The Coffee Bean, to name just a few. So, the next time you need a little jolt of joe to get you through an early-morning meeting or a late-night

GRE study session, step up to the counter, look the barista right in the eye, and just say *decaf.*

THE SHOW: *My So-Called Life*

A BRIEF REFRESHER: Arguably one of the greatest depictions of teen angst on the small screen, like, evah (we also gotta give *Freaks and Geeks* mad props, but it aired too late to make this list), painfully short-lived *My So-Called Life* chronicles the sighs and longing stares of scarlet-haired protagonist Angela Chase (Claire Danes), who was too smart and introspective (or was it clinically depressed?) for her own good. (FYI: We're breaking character and abandoning the royal *we* for a moment to make very important announcement. Back in the day of combat boots paired with flowered dresses, one of the authors of this book—hint: her name rhymes with "Nessica"—attempted to home-dye her hair "Angela Chase red" and instead ended up with "Dame Edna pink." Let this be a lesson: Sun-In and Clairol Natural Instincts don't mix. Now back to our regularly scheduled use of *we.* . . .) Angela rolled with a posse that included wild child latchkey kid Rayanne Graff and gay bestie Rickie, and she lusted over beautiful slow-learner Jordan Catalano (Jared Leto), who was sex on a stick—that is, if the stick happened to rock a flannel shirt and have shaggy, soft, touchable hair. Of course, nothing in the world of adolescence is ever simple, so *My So-Called Life* offers up lots of inner turmoil, sex, drugs, and unrequited love.

WHAT YOU CAN LEARN FROM THIS SHOW TODAY: Speaking of unrequited love, who can forget the agony and heartache of Brian Krakow, the geeky boy next door who carries a flame for Angela Chase that burns as brightly as her hair? He even pulls a Cyrano de Bergerac, penning steamy letters to his beloved and passing them off as the work of the empty, beautiful vessel that was Jordan. If, after all of these years, you're still harboring a bad-boy fascination that's getting in the way of finding a guy who treats you right, try giving a good guy a chance. Who knows the depths of passion that could lie below his clean-cut exterior? Plus, even though Mr. So-Wrong-He's-Right always looks dangerously hot as he leans against his high school locker, lost in what you imagined were intense thoughts about life and love, in reality, he probably isn't actually thinking about anything at all. Except maybe boobies. Today, he might not be leaning against the high school lockers (he's graduated to standing at the bar), but your bad boy is still thinking about boobies. (OK, to be fair, he might also be thinking about his fantasy football team—and boobies.)

THE SHOW: *Blossom*

A BRIEF REFRESHER: Those hats! (So floppy and fabulous!) That name! (*I'm a bialy? Mayan ball lick? Me llamo a Miami?*) That brother! (No, not Tony, the former drug addict. We're talking about Joey Lawrence, back when he rocked wavy nineties heartthrob hair.) Today, *Blossom* signifies days of television gone by, a time when teen stars were endearing, quirky, real, and admittedly a bit corny, rather than dolled-up, branded, handled, and Photoshopped (and Pixy Stix thin—here's looking at you, cast of *90210* redux.) Mayim Bialik played the title character of this series, who—surprise, surprise—is raised by her dad after her mother jumps ship, because if you believed everything you watched in the sitcoms, maternal abandonment, not crack, was the true epidemic of the late eighties and early nineties. Blossom's dad is a musician, a real hip guy who plays gigs in between raising Blossom and her aforementioned brothers: the twelve-stepper Anthony and the dopey puppy dog Joey, who was a lot like that hot guy you dated in ninth grade way longer than you should have due to his kissing skills, rather than his beautiful mind. (He thought Las Vegas was a state.) Blossom, err, blossoms into a full-blown teenager, along with Six, her pint-sized bestie who chatters like a speed freak.

WHAT YOU CAN LEARN FROM THIS SHOW TODAY: We don't know about you, but one of the most heartbreaking moments of 2009 was when Mayim Bialik surrendered to the makeover show *What Not to Wear*. Yes, we're well aware that a grown-up Mayim and the adolescent character she played on an early nineties sitcom are two very different people (one of which is not even real), but just the thought of our beloved Blossom trading in her Doc Martens and baby-doll dresses for Nine West pumps and a closet full of Ann Taylor separates makes us want to wear a floppy hat with a giant sunflower in protest. Our point: If you have a quirky sense of style, more power to you, and don't let any so-called experts tell you otherwise. It doesn't matter if you're a big girl. You can still retain some sense of originality. Hell, let your fashion freak flag fly—as long as it won't get you in trouble with the HR department. (If that's the case, you might want to save your more "unique" outfits for your days off.)

THE SHOW: *Beverly Hills, 90210*

A BRIEF REFRESHER COURSE: Let's just get one thing straight. When it comes to *90210*, "The Brenda Years" are the *only* years that matter and we're not even going to acknowledge the disgrace of a teen soap opera that followed her untimely departure. Whew! Now that we got that out of the way, cue up the "da-na-na-na, da-na-na-na" theme song and let the memories flood back to you. One day you're kicking it with your mom-jeans-wearing twin brother, Brandon, in Minnesota, just, like, enjoying the seasons and stuff when your dad gets a promotion and makes the family move to Beverly Hills. ("Pack up the station wagon, Cindy!") Like any good Midwestern girl, Brenda Walsh (Shannen Doherty) experiences a bit of culture shock (Beemers in the school parking lot, coke-snorting parents, and a fun little game called Skeletons in the Closet!). Not that you need a refresher course on the crew that the Walsh kids roll with (if you do, we're assuming you grew up Amish or something), but just for fun, let's do a little West Beverly High roll call. There's Kelly Taylor (Jennie Garth), the beautiful blonde (at least she was after her nose job); Donna Martin (Tori Spelling), the neuroscientist who never meets a crop top she doesn't love; Andrea Zuckerman (Gabrielle Carteris), the septuagenarian who doesn't even, like, live in the school district; Dylan McKay (Luke Perry), the brooding heartthrob with killer sideburns; Steve Sanders (Ian Ziering), the ultimate douche bag (need we remind you that the license plate on his Corvette reads "I8A 4RE"?); and David Silver (Brian Austin Green), Casio keyboard master. Now, back to Brenda. . . . Things get really good with her character when she starts dating Dylan, to whom she eventually loses her virginity at the Spring Fling dance after making him wait a full five episodes. Despite a pregnancy scare, Brenda and Dylan's relationship gets *way* serious—so serious in fact that Jim and Cindy ship her off to Paris, an act that results in one of TV's greatest love triangles. Ultimately, Dylan and Kelly confess to their sordid affair, prompting Brenda to scream, "I hate both of you! Never talk to me again!" and torch her old photos while blaring R.E.M.'s "Losing My Religion." Post-graduation, things go kind of downhill for Brenda: a failed stint at University of Minnesota, a broken engagement to Stuart Carson, involvement with a radical animal activist group. Ultimately, Brenda hightails it to London, where she receives a scholarship to the Royal Academy of Dramatic Art (what—you've never heard of RADA?) only to get replaced by Kelly Kapowski from *Saved by the Bell*.

WHAT YOU CAN LEARN FROM THE SHOW TODAY: What *can't* you learn from the show today? For starters, you're never too old to play a teenager on television (right, AHN-drea?). Brenda alone provides a slew of life lessons, including how to get laid while visiting a foreign country (duh, adopt a terrible fake accent and seduce a dumb yet smoking-hot tourist). But perhaps the biggest takeaway is the importance of loyalty when it comes to friendship. Sure, it's necessary to meet new and exciting people, but don't forget the nurture your relationships with the good old standbys, the ones who have always been there for you. Just ask Donna, who might not be permitted to graduate from high school as punishment for being totally smashed at the prom. Luckily, her good pal Brandon Walsh springs into action, leading a schoolwide walkout during finals in which the students chant, "Donna Martin graduates! Donna Martin graduates!" Best. Television. Moment. Ever.

THE SHOW: *The Wonder Years*

A BRIEF REFRESHER: The show centers around Kevin Arnold (played by *Tiger Beat* cover favorite Fred Savage), a baby-faced adolescent coming of age in the late sixties, as narrated by a nostalgic grown-up Kevin (voiced by the original Gossip Girl, Daniel Stern). Kevin's family includes his disgruntled father, stay-at-home mom, absentee hippie sister, and psychotic brother. (How much did you hate Wayne?) But Kevin's main source of teen angst is his tumultuous relationship with Winnie Cooper, the girl next door with the waist-length hair. The two share their first kiss in the pilot episode after her brother dies in Vietnam and Kevin gives her his New York Jets jacket to keep her warm (cue "When a Man Loves a Woman"). But things cool off when Winnie magically develops a set of mini-boobs before the first day of junior high, thereby making her wet dream material (eww, we can't believe we just went there), and starts dating an eighth grader. In an attempt to move on, Kevin romances Becky Slater, a mentally unstable blonde who sucker-punches him twice when he breaks up with her. ("Friends?! I'll give you friends!") Then, in a totally uncool move, Winnie briefly dates Kevin's geek-tastic best friend, Paul Pfeiffer (who for the last time was not, we repeat NOT, played by Marilyn Manson). But don't cry for K-dog because he manages to hook up with some major hotties, including Lisa Berlini (who ditches him for some beefcake named Brad, played by real-life beefcake Mark-Paul Gosselaar, a.k.a. Zack Morris) and Madeline Adams, a teen French seductress. But it is Winnie who Kevin wants, and it is widely believed that during the final episode the two finally seal the deal. (Remember, this was a family show so all we got was some kissing and a shared blanket.)

WHAT YOU CAN LEARN FROM THIS SHOW TODAY: As far as happy endings go (and no, we don't mean the kind sleazy guys get at shady massage parlors), *The Wonder Years* was a huge letdown. One would assume that Kevin and Winnie end up getting married and going on to have lots of mini Winnies, but actually, Daniel Stern slips it in the final epilogue that it doesn't go down quite like that. Winnie moves to Paris for eight years and, while she and Kevin stay friends, he ends up marrying someone else. Here's the thing: Winnie is the ultimate commitment-phobe. She toys with Kevin's heart for a *long* time, and perhaps he finally grows a pair and moves on. The life lesson is this: Sometimes, something that feels like "true love" isn't actually meant to be. Life really isn't a fairy tale. Don't fret if your life takes a path that's much different than you could have ever anticipated. Things often have a way of working out via surprise endings. Case in point: In real life, big brother Wayne married a porn star. Who woulda thunk?

Nine

Ladies Who Lunch Versus Girls' Night Out: Your Ever-Evolving Social Circle

Friendship is born at that moment when one person says to another, "What! You too? I thought I was the only one."

—C. S. Lewis

BEST FRIENDS 4-EVA

Whoever said "Strangers are friends we haven't met yet" obviously never rode on a city bus during rush hour or attempted to maneuver through a traffic jam. (Up yours, too, buddy!) Probably never had to contend with any of the other inconveniences of modern-day life, either, like jam-packed calendars and endless hours of overtime. Our obsession with overextension, combined with the fact that we're experiencing major upheaval right now, means one thing for making and maintaining friendships during the redo-berty years: It sure as hell ain't as easy as it used to be. Today, if we fail to clear room in our busy schedules for each other, even our closest pals are in danger of becoming nothing more than strangers on the bus (we swear we're not trying to rip off that Joan Osborne song).

OK, so making friends used to be easier, but puberty wasn't exactly a picnic when it came to your social life. There were the petty fights, the cliques, the bullies, the angst, and the fact that kids are cruel—or maybe we should say they're more upfront about their cruelty than we adults are.

On the brighter side, you didn't have to venture much further than homeroom to find common ground with your peers. Your closest friends were the ones who were literally the closest to you—you shared a lunch table, lived on the same block, wore matching softball uniforms, and goofed off during ballet class, giggling your way through demi-pliés at Miss Debbie's Dance Studio. Your worries, interests, and life experiences generally matched up with your friends' worries, interests, and life experiences. Going to school, awkwardly flirting with boys, enduring parents who just didn't understand, and trying to figure out how you fit in with the rest of the world—these were your favorite things, the glue that held friendships together.

Sure, there was always the odd girl in the group who sprinted ahead of everyone else in the game of life, like underage vixen Vanessa Taylor, she of the Playboy-worthy rack and burgeoning libido, who let "Hot" Scott Sadowsky (you may remember him from Chapter 5, "Hooking Up, Shacking Up, and Marrying Up: The State of Your Love Life") fumble his way to second base—underneath her D-cup bra, no less—in Heather Wiener's basement after the Spring Fling dance. It was a scandalous move considering that no one else in your group had even gotten a real kiss yet. (Thanks to the beauty of Facebook, you now know that Vanessa has three children, a big house with a yard, and, from the looks of her pageant-worthy coif, an obsession with the Bumpit, the amazing as-seen-on-TV hairdoodad that takes your locks from flat to fabulous.)

Even during your early twenties, your friends' life trajectories tended to match up with your own. You worked, you went out on the town, you looked for love, you endured heartbreak, you shared crappy apartments, and you transitioned into young adulthood together. You had everything in common. And then you grew up—for real.

The New Coming of Age Moments: The Friend Edition

Before we go into why your friendships get hit the hardest during your redo-berty years, let's take a look back at a time when you and your BFF talked on the phone every night for no less than two hours.

Puberty	Redo-berty
Reading the Baby-Sitters Club books with your friends	Baby-sitting your friends' kids
Your so-called best friend steals your boyfriend.	Your so-called best friend steals your baby name.
You confess to your BFF that you got to third base with your boyfriend.	Your BFF confesses to you that she hasn't had sex with her husband in three months.
You're not allowed to call her past 10 p.m. or you'll wake up her parents.	You're not allowed to call her past 10 p.m. or you'll wake up her baby.
Agonizing over which friends should be on your speed dial	Agonizing over which friends should be in your bridal party
Taking gymnastics classes with your BFF	Doing Weight Watchers with your BFF
Wearing best friend necklaces	Listing each other as your emergency contact
Dressing up as Care Bears (Grumpy Bear, Love-a-Lot Bear, Friend Bear, and Bedtime Bear) for Halloween with your barely pubescent posse	Dressing up as "slutty" Care Bears (Humpy Bear, Me-Love-You-Long-Time Bear, Friends-with-Benefits Bear, and, naturally, Bedtime Bear) with your too-old-for-this posse for Halloween
Passing notes in class	Sending BBMs at work
Making each other mix tapes	Burning each other CDs

Once the redo-berty years hit, everything changes. Marriage, families, careers—as members of your posse grow up, get knocked up, and move up, friendships inevitably evolve. And, just like the *P* word (which is *puberty*, in case you forgot), all of these changes are only natural. You'll make new friends and drift away from some of the old ones. You'll also grapple with busy schedules, geographic barriers, and occasional feelings of loneliness, despite the fact that you have 724 Facebook friends. That's the bad news. The good news is this: As long as you put forth the effort, your friendships can be stronger than ever. We need our pals, our confidantes, our ladies (and guys) to share the good times and the bad, the ups and the downs. Now, let's get together, have a group hug, and then go out for cosmos. Actually, first, before we down pink beverages that look pretty but taste like an embarrassing display on the dance floor followed by a late-night drunken sobbing session about your ex-boyfriend, take a look at some likely states of your social circle today.

Some Possible Scenarios: Where You're at with Your Friend-ships

ALONE IN THE CROWD: You've got a healthy roster of Facebook pals, a long list of email contacts, and a cell phone address book that's packed with other people's digits. However, when it comes to real friends—you know, the ones you actually see in real life—you feel like a lone ranger. You're surrounded by acquaintances but lacking true confidantes. Blame it on our modern-day conveniences. Nowadays, it's way easier to text rather than talk, break plans rather than make them, and virtually "poke" rather than reach out and touch somebody (in a totally un-pervy sort of way, of course). The only cure for real-friend deficiency is to get out there and pursue actual relationships. Use technology to your advantage to reconnect with virtual buddies in real life. Or join a club, cultivate your passions, and basically get off the couch and venture out there into the big and not-always-so-bad world. (For more on what to do if you have a bunch of acquaintances but no close friends, see the "Adult Education" section of this chapter.)

FEELING LEFT OUT: Whether you're like ample-bosomed Vanessa Taylor, who let Scott Sadowsky cop the feel that launched a pre-pubescent scandal, or you're a Judy Blume–style late boomer, it can suck if you feel out of step with your group of friends. Perhaps you're married with children in a sea of unpartnered pals or you're single and ready to mingle while the rest of your tribe prefers nice little Saturdays at Bed Bath & Beyond with their significant others. Here's a word of advice if you're feeling angsty or lonely after venturing into uncharted water outside of your social circle: Grow up. It may sound harsh, but change is part of being an adult. In fact, here's a major plot twist: Your friends shouldn't all look, act, and talk alike. Remember, variety is the spice of life, and clones are only cool in sci-fi movies.

THE NEW GIRL IN TOWN: Let's go back in time once again. Think back to middle school, when halfway through the year, your home-room teacher announced that a new student was joining the class. Technically, there was nothing *wrong* with Kimberly Goodman (other than the fact that she called soda "pop" and sprinkles "jim-mies"), but for whatever reason, you and your crew never invited her to sit at your lunch table or asked her if she wanted to hang out after school. Well, it looks like the only thing bitchier than seventh grade girls is karma. Whether you made a big move to go back to school, seize a new job opportunity, or follow your significant other, being the new girl in town is one of life's loneliest experiences. Sure, you might have a few phone numbers and emails of locals that were passed on by friends, but contacting a total stranger to see if she wants to go out for sushi is way scarier than asking a guy on a date. As we've said already (and we'll repeat later in this chapter), making friends gets harder the older you get, especially when you're starting from scratch. (For more advice on that, see Burning Question #1 in the "Adult Education" section.) In the meantime, you should look up Kimberly Goodman on Facebook and see what she's up to these days (perhaps she's rocking the Bumpit like Vanessa Taylor).

STUCK WITH A FRENEMY: At one time or another every woman has to deal with a toxic friend. Maybe she's the type of person who cancels plans at the last minute and doesn't even try to come up with believable excuses (we've yet to meet someone who got food poisoning from Pinkberry). Or perhaps this so-called friend's neurons aren't firing correctly and she attacks you with a Christian Bale–style rant after you don't reply to a text right away even though she sent it at 2 a.m. on a Wednesday. How your frenemy (part friend, part enemy) goes about tormenting you isn't even the issue. What's most important is that all of her drama is making you feel like a character in a scripted reality show where every week's episode is the "most shocking one yet." Frankly, you're freaking exhausted. You know that life is too short to waste on negative people, yet you tolerate this "friend's" borderline behavior. We'd ask you why, but we're pretty sure we know what the answer is: Either you're worried that giving her the boot will make you look like a bad person (talk about ironic) or you're scared that the only thing worse than being her friend is being on her bad side. Well, if you decide to finally cut her free (and we really hope that you do), moral support is waiting for you in Burning Question #3 in the "Adult Education" section.

What's Really Going on When It Comes to Your Circle of Friends: A Little Psychological Perspective

Our resident expert, Dr. Kevin Brennan, weighs in with one of the reasons why making and maintaining relationships with our confidantes is harder during the redo-berty years. Of course, we have busier lives than we used to in our early twenties, but our quest for perfection also plays a role in undermining our platonic relationships.

"We're so focused on making it that we load up on responsibilities and don't have time for the effort with friends," he says.

There's an easy way to fix this: Make yourself find the time to put in the effort with your friends. With social networking sites and iEverythings, keeping in touch shouldn't be a problem.

On a positive note about friendship during this day and age, Dr. Kevin brings up a great point about Facebook: It lets us really get to know each other. "Our parents didn't know their friends like we do," says Dr. Kevin. "The fact that we now have so much knowledge about our friends means we can chose who we keep close."

Now, let's all take a break and view our News Feeds.

Adult Education: Experts Answer Your Most Burning Friendship Questions

Wouldn't it be nice if female friendships were just like the ones you see on commercials for Yaz, yogurt, and air freshener? You know how it goes: A group of equally attractive women sit around a table and share their innermost feelings while never *ever* silently judging one another's life choices. In reality, female friendships are just slightly more complicated than the way they appear in the soft light of daytime television ads, especially now when it feels like everyone you're close with is hitting the major adult milestones—marriage, babies, and mortgages—at different times, making it harder than ever to find common ground.

Unlike some of the other chapters in this book, where we shrugged our shoulders and passed the buck to the real experts, we're actually going to take the reins on this one. See, we're also the authors of *Friend or Frenemy?: A Guide to the Friends You Need and the Ones You Don't.* And just in case you wanted a second opinion (no offense taken), we also enlisted the help of Dr. Irene S. Levine, author of *Best Friends Forever: Surviving a Breakup with Your Best Friend.* Thanks to the three of us, all your friend woes should be covered.

Burning Question #1: I've watched just about all of the Lifetime movies a girl can handle. How can I meet new people, especially during the redo-berty years, when it seems so many are already set with their own lives and groups of friends?

Like we mentioned earlier in this chapter, it used to be so much easier to make new friends. Girl meets girl, girl shares her My Little Pony with other girl, and a lifelong friendship is born (well, at least until middle school, when one half of the friendly duo fills out a D-cup a la Vanessa Taylor and the other is relegated to wearing undershirts from the girl's department at JCPenney).

The sad truth is that the older you get, the more your responsibilities pile up in your personal and professional lives, and the harder it is to make true friends. When you're in your late twenties and early thirties, marriages and families are often in their early stages, and it can feel like no one has the time for some good old-fashioned socializing. While it's true that your friendships aren't going to be as simple as they were during your adolescence, they are still an important part of your life. If you connect with someone, don't rule her out as a friend if she has a life that's very different from yours (for example, she's married with kids and you're single and ready to mingle, or vice versa). Think of it a lot like dating: If you go into a situation with a defeatist attitude, you could push away potential pals. The key is to keep an open mind. And, also much like dating, you're not going to meet any potential friends if you stay in on Saturday night to wash your hair and Bioré-strip your pores.

Amazingly enough, the first step to meeting people is to actually go out and meet them. You need to leave the house and get in some face time with other women, says Dr. Levine. Not sure where to find all these potential new pals? Follow your interests and enroll yourself in a class or an activity where you'll meet other like-minded ladies. It also helps to smile and strike up a conversation with the woman next to you in Pilates class, in the pedi chair at the salon, or even in the cubicle at work (shockingly, some people actually enjoy spending time with their coworkers outside of the office). These steps might sound obvious, but as Levine points out, it's important to come off as warm and open, especially since shyness can be mistaken for aloofness. Start with a simple "Hi" and work your way up to small talk until you feel confident enough to move into "Do you know a good gynecologist?" territory.

Another simple yet effective suggestion is to fall into a routine. "When you do anything regularly, seeing the same person or people time after time, you'll make acquaintances who can morph into friends over time," says Levine.

And just for the record, we love us some Lifetime programming and would be happy to sit next to you on the couch during the next "Stalked by a Lover Sunday" or "Secrets and Seduction Saturday."

Burning Question #2: My friend recently got engaged to a guy that I really, really don't like. Should I tell her that I think she's making a big mistake hitching her wagon to such a douche bag?

You know the part of the wedding ceremony where the officiant says,

"If any of you can show just cause why they may not lawfully be married, speak now; or else for ever hold your peace"? That's your cue to stand up and announce that the groom grabbed your ass at a party last New Year's Eve, has three baby mamas, and wears Ed Hardy shirts (that last one will surely elicit gasps from the crowd). We guarantee that your friend will be so touched by your genuine concern for her well-being that you'll get to take her ex-fiancé's place on the honeymoon and the two of you will sip piña coladas and relax on the white sands of the Caribbean knowing that a disaster was averted.

Okay, let's get serious. This is an extremely delicate situation, and one you're bound to face during your so-called life, when it seems like there's a wedding every weekend. Good friends are *supposed* to be honest with each other, but when it comes down to it, no one ever *really* wants to hear the truth. Your friend doesn't want to be told that those skinny jeans make her butt look anything but skinny, and she really doesn't want to know that her husband-to-be makes Joe "Girls Gone Wild" Francis seem like a nice young man. So, tread lightly when it comes to criticism.

"You don't want to put her in a situation where she feels like she's being judged or worse—that she has to choose between you and him," says Dr. Levine.

For this reason, we actually advise against speaking up about a friend's significant other, unless, of course, the relationship is abusive or truly toxic. (If that's the case, then you have our permission to get all Dr. Phil on her ass.) But, be prepared to face the fact that once you let your opinion be known, anything can happen to your friendship. Best-case scenario: Your pal will realize on her own that her man is a total loser and then you can break out the champagne and toast to hoes before bros and all that girl-power stuff. Worst-case scenario: She'll unleash a tirade on you that will rival the time when Theresa from *The Real Housewives of New Jersey* flipped over the table during a classy dinner. ("Prostitution Whore" is still one of our favorite insults of all time.)

Burning Question #3: Is it ever OK to break up with a friend? If so, how do I do it?

We're about to let you in on a dirty little secret: Best friends aren't always forever. This truth can be hard to accept because we've always been taught that women are supposed to stick together like Thelma and Louise (only without the double suicide at the end). Just like the flames of passion can burn out in a romantic relationship, the bonds that hold a friendship together can become unglued, leaving you wondering if it's time to cut ties. Sometimes, like puberty, it's only natural. You're an adult now, and old enough to realize that people change and friendships can sink. To help you figure things out, steal a move from the traditional breakup playbook and take some space, or what Dr. Levine calls a "friendship sabbatical," which leaves the door to your relationship open.

"Time apart may make you realize that you really don't want to end it or that you've lost nothing being apart," she says.

If it becomes clear that the friendship is sinking and that a breakup is the way to go, the best way to do it is face to face. Oh, who are we kidding? That's *so* not happening. As women, we're conditioned to avoid confrontation and we would rather hold in our true feelings than actually sit down with a friend and explain that the relationship isn't working for us. Even Levine admits that it's easier to make up an excuse or tell a white lie. ("I've joined a cult" always works for us.) Why unnecessarily hurt someone who once was your close friend?

Burning Question #4: I have a lot of acquaintances but no real close friends. How can I make my friendships more meaningful?

According to a semi-recent study, the key to happiness is having at least ten good friends. Assuming that there is truth to these findings, we don't blame you for wanting to launch *America's Next Top BFF*, a reality show where contestants compete to be a part of your inner circle. (We imagine that the challenges would be something like "Hair-Braiding" and "Prank-Calling Boys.")

The irony of the digital age is that while it allows us to make connections with new people every day, it can also limit the quality of these relationships, and what ends up happening is that you have tons of "friends" wishing you a happy birthday on your Facebook wall but no one to actually take you out to celebrate. When it comes to forging authentic friendships, you have to do less of the superficial stuff and pursue more of the good old-fashioned face-to-face connections. We probably sound like a broken record here, but it's worth mentioning again: We're busy adults, and during your redo-berty years, you're going to have to put in more effort to maintain your friendships. It's as simple (or as hard) as that.

"Relationships are based on intimacy and trust, which can only be achieved with time and experience," says Dr. Levine. She suggests choosing one or two people from your pool of acquaintances that you want to get to know better and gradually start hanging out with them more often. But be careful not to get all Lennie from *Of Mice and Men* on your pals and stifle them with too much love and affection. The process is gradual and you shouldn't expect too much too soon. And speaking of expectations, keep in mind that not everyone is fortunate enough to find the gold standard of friendship: the best friend. You may end up with a few good friends that compliment different aspects of your personality. And that's totally normal. Oh, and about that study we mentioned earlier—don't worry so much about filling up ten slots with shiny new BFFs. According to one of the researchers, the main finding from the research is that actively working on your friendships is a prerequisite for happiness.

Burning Question #5: I used to have so much in common with my friends, but now we're all at different places in our lives. How can we stay connected?

Back in college and your early twenties, you and your friends did so much together that they became your second family (or "framily," as we like to call it). As you enter the redo-berty years, something amazing happens: Your friends start building real families of their own (not to mention embarking on new careers), thereby limiting the amount of things you have in common and the time you have to hang out.

While it's totally normal for your friendships to fluctuate at different life stages, it doesn't mean you should let your uber-busy schedules or increased responsibilities ruin your most important relationships, says Dr. Levine. "Friendships, especially old ones, are like scrapbooks containing the memories of our lives, and they are worth preserving," she adds. (If that doesn't belong embroidered on a pillow, then we don't know what does.)

The easiest way to stay connected to your pals, especially if they don't live in the same city as you, is digitally—via email, texts, IM, Facebook, etc. But keep in mind that these instant forms of communication are like low-fat ice cream: temporarily satisfying but not nearly as good as the real deal. "Try to create rituals for getting together and sharing what you do have in common," says Dr. Levine. She suggests scheduling a standing girls' night out.

One last thing that should go without saying, but we're going to say it anyway, is this: Make it a point to remember the significant days in your friends' lives (such as their birthdays, their kids' birthdays, and anniversaries) and be there when they really need you (during breakups, deaths, illnesses, and other not-so-fun stuff—the real-life scenarios that you'll all start to face during your so-called life). Remember: Genuine connections aren't just about brunching, gossiping, and going out. That's what is known as a fair-weather friendship or an episode of *The Hills*.

UNFRIENDLY ADVICE:
YOU'RE NOT A TOTAL FREAK IF YOU DON'T . . .

Women's magazines love feel-good stories with titles like "The 10 Friends Every Woman Needs." Come to think of it, they like a lot of stories that tell women what they need, crave, and desire. Well, we wanted to change things up a bit. Below, we list some social interactions that you don't need to crave or desire in order to be normal.

YOU'RE NOT A TOTAL FREAK IF YOU DON'T . . .

1. **Roll with a posse that rivals a rapper:** You're an adult now, and you should have left the cliques back in high school where they belong. Sometimes people—surprise, surprise—have different interests and don't want to go along with the group all of the time. That being said, it's perfectly healthy if you have a la carte friendships, confidantes from different aspects of your life, who don't all roll up together into da club.

2. **Have a Will to your Grace:** This may come as a big surprise, but gay men are people, not cheerleaders who exist only to make straight women feel fabulous.

3. **Have a Dawson to your Joey:** Of course women can have guy friends, but the simple fact is that the older you get, the harder it is to find a straight man who puts up with listening to all of your deepest darkest secrets and doesn't want to sleep with you.

4. **Mix business with pleasure:** While you should be on polite terms with your coworkers, there's nothing wrong with leaving the office at the office at the end of the day and keeping your social life separate from happy hour at T.G.I. Friday's with Marge in accounting.

5. **Have a BFF:** Maybe you're lucky and have so many close friends that you can't just choose one to be your best one. Or perhaps you're shy or new in town and looking to expand your social circle. Or, even better, maybe your significant other is your best friend, which is really cute. No, really, it is.

IN CONCLUSION

We need our friends more than ever. Sure, some of us might be married now and have our own families, but that doesn't mean that our social universe needs to implode. With some extra effort and understanding, our friendships during the redo-berty years can weather the ups and downs of this second puberty. (And yup, the *P* word is still gross.)

1. People change and grow apart. It's only natural. Not all friendships are meant to last forever.
2. If you don't like your friend's significant other/husband, it might be best to tread lightly unless she's stuck in an abusive situation. If that's the case, then go all UFC on his ass.
3. Think of trying to make new friends like dating: Keep an open mind, manage your expectations, find people who share your interests, and get up off the couch and out there.
4. Now that you've reached your redo-berty years, you have to realize that friendships take more effort to maintain, but they're totally worth it.
5. You're an adult now. It's totally normal if you don't roll deep. We promise.

Signs That Your Friendship Is All Grown Up

You two go way back. Perhaps you bonded in the dorms or, even better, maybe you became friends while wearing swimmies and diapers, splashing about in the water as your moms bonded in baby aqua-aerobics class. No matter how you met, you've been through it all together—the ups, the downs, the good times and the bad. Even though you've been friends for years, sometimes it takes a big-girl moment to realize that you aren't little kids anymore. Here are some signs that your relationship is maturing.

1. She whips out her boob and starts breastfeeding during brunch. And yes, that was her nipple.
2. She invites you over to see her new refinished floors
3. You go on vacation together and don't sleep in the same bed.
4. You list your BFF as your emergency contact instead of your mom.
5. She sends you one of those photo holiday cards where everyone, including the golden retriever, looks deliriously happy.
6. When you dial her up at the office, her assistant has to put your call through.
7. She becomes a Republican (or "fiscal conservative," as she calls it).
8. You email her an article about stroller safety from *Consumer Reports*.
9. You organize a wine tasting instead of a pub crawl for her birthday.
10. You sign up for a spin class together . . . on a Sunday . . . at 9 a.m.

Sounding Off

Chances are that in your younger years, you assumed that by your thirtieth birthday you'd have at least one of the following: a husband with all of his hair, a fulfilling career, and one of those babies that never cries. Oh, to be twenty-two and naïve again. Our ladies gave it to us straight when we threw out this question: **What do you think you'd be doing at this age?**

"When I was about five, I probably thought I'd be dead or a mermaid. When I was in college, I thought I'd be living a yuppie lifestyle with an MBA or a law degree."—*Jen, 26*

"I thought I'd be married to a successful doctor/banker/lawyer-type man, pregnant, working for the U.N., and living in a house fifty times larger than my current NYC studio."—*Alix, 28*

"I absolutely thought I'd be married with at least one child by now."—*Julie, 29*

"When I was little, thirty seemed ancient to me. I thought by twenty-five I would be married with kids. But once I got to college, I knew I wouldn't be 'that girl' getting married right out of school. I didn't want to be part of the divorce epidemic. I'm not saying all people who get married in their early twenties are destined to break up, but let's be honest, who the hell knows who they are or what they want at twenty-three?"—*Melissa, 30*

"I thought I'd be a crusading newspaper journalist doing hard-hitting interviews and writing stirring op-eds. But, you know, newspapers are dead, so I have a Wordpress blog where I write about what I ate for brunch. It's probably going to be short-listed for the Pulitzer this year."—*Sara, 28*

"I thought I'd be making a living as a performance artist instead of juggling performing with a soul-sucking office job."—*Carla, 27*

"When I was a kid I'm sure I thought I'd be married with kids by now . . . but then, as I kept getting older, I always seemed too young to be married, let alone married with kids. Finally, around my thirtieth birthday, I realized I was ready."—*Laura, 32.5*

"Exactly what I'm doing now: teaching, owning a house, married, and starting a family."—*Candice, 31*

"What I am now, but richer in both the financial sense and the family sense, which means having a house full of children and eventually grandchildren."—*Megan, 30*

"I'm exactly what I thought I would be by thirty: a mom."—*Lori, 30*

"I was entertaining the idea of being a nun."—*Danielle, 26*

Ten

Renter, Owner, or Squatter: A Place to Call Home

Cady: Wow. Your house is really nice.
Regina: I know, right?

—from *Mean Girls*

BED BATH & WAY BEYOND

Like nails on a chalkboard or the sound of Paris Hilton's fake Betty Boop voice, the word "nesting" gives us the heebie-jeebies (maybe because it also conjures up images of rodents, hornets, and other unwanted critters that warrant a visit from the friendly neighborhood exterminator). Unfortunately, just like one of those suburban methhead moms on *Intervention*, we have a dangerous habit that we can't control. *Nesting, nesting, nesting!*

Thanks to the popularity of HGTV, blankets with sleeves, and staycations, the N word is all the rage these days. Why emerge from the *nest* and participate in the world when you can roll yourself up into a polyester-blend Snuggie/Slanket/snafghan cocoon? That being said, this chapter is all about the place you call "home." Whether it's a one-room apartment, a five-bedroom McMansion, or a suite at the Chateau Marmont, we all need a safe space where we can unwind and be ourselves away from the prying eyes of everyone else. (Just make sure that your creepy landlord doesn't install a spy cam in your attic a la the classic Lifetime movie *Video Voyeur: The Susan Wilson Story*, starring Angie Harmon.)

In addition to the emergence of *nesting, nesting, nesting* (we can stop whenever we want—we swear!) as a cultural phenomenon, something rather curious (actually, maybe it's not so curious) happens once you reach the redo-berty years: Painting the town red on a nightly basis no longer has the appeal it once did. Today, you catch yourself saying things like "I don't like to sleep in late because then half the day is gone," or "Why is it so loud in here?" (Answer: Because it's a bar.) Remember when the weekend actually began at happy hour on Thursday and your weekend mornings actually began at noon? Or, think back even further to your adolescence, when you would rather have sported orthodontic headgear in public than spend a Friday night at home on the sofa watching *20/20* with Mom and Dad (unless you were lucky enough to have the type of misguided parents who preferred that you and your friends imbibe under their own roof—"I'm not a regular mom! I'm a cool mom!"—rather than knock back bottles of wine coolers with the other high school delinquents in the woods near the old water tower).

The New Coming of Age Moments: Home Sweet Home Edition

Your bedroom used to be quite the versatile space. At once, it was a haven from bratty siblings and hovering parents, a place to daydream about getting out of this god-awful town, and when you sassed your parents it was your jail cell. Today, the idea of getting grounded sounds downright relaxing (isn't it called a staycation?), but your home still serves a similar function to your adolescent years. It's your refuge from the craziness of the daily grind, your safe space, and an expression of your creativity.

Puberty	Redo-berty
Stashing your diary in your underwear drawer	Stashing your vibrator in your underwear drawer
Hanging a Boyz II Men poster on your wall	Downloading "Motown Philly" from iTunes
Snuggling up with your twelve besties in sleeping bags in the living room during a sleepover	Kindly telling your deadbeat friend, who's been snuggling up on your couch for three months, that it's time for her to find other accommodations
Flunking your geometry final and losing your phone privileges for a week	Flunking your, um, mortgage payments and losing your home privileges
Practicing the Running Man and the Roger Rabbit in front of your bedroom mirror while listening to "Pump Up the Jam"	Practicing the moves from the *Dancing with the Stars: Latin Cardio Dance* DVD
Yelling at your brother for taking your Victoria's Secret catalogs into the bathroom with him when he goes number two	Yelling at your boyfriend for taking your Victoria's Secret catalogs into the bathroom with him when he goes number two
Cleaning your room by shoving all of your crap into the closet and under your bed	Cleaning your apartment by pushing a Swiffer around for a few minutes
Complaining to your mother because she never "buys anything good" at the supermarket (and by "anything good," you mean potato chips, pizza rolls, and ice cream sandwiches)	Complaining to your husband because he keeps too much junk food around the house (and by "junk food," you mean potato chips, pizza rolls, and ice cream sandwiches)

Puberty	Redo-berty
Having friends over to play Sega Genesis	Having friend over to play *Rock Band*
Begging your parents for your own phone line in your room	Getting rid of your landline because you never use it

Today, there's something empowering about turning down plans and staying in because you want to recharge and wake up without feeling (or smelling) like you spent the night in a frat house.

We guess an easier way to say this is that you—surprise, surprise—grow up and have new priorities—you know, *shit to do*. And a major part of growing up involves your pad, your casa, your digs. Unlike in college and your early twenties, when anything over four hundred square feet was considered practically palatial, the playing field is no longer level during the redo-berty years. In fact, it's more like a throwback to middle school when you were insanely jealous of Angela Valenti because she had an in-ground pool, a hot tub, *and* cabinets that were always stocked with junk food like Pringles, Laffy Taffy, and Easy Cheese. (That girl was one model train in the living room away from being Ricky Stratton on *Silver Spoons*.) When you get older, it's more likely that your friends' living situations will be vastly different than your own. Sorry to kill the fantasy of bunking together in Monica Geller's massive rent-controlled apartment, which just happens to be across the hall from your two best (non-gay) guy friends. Read on to find out where you fit in.

Some Likely Scenarios: Where You're at with Your Pad

GOING SOLO: After sharing living space with a parade of roommates (some pleasant, some neurotic, and others full-on psychotic), you're a big girl, and you've finally made the big-girl leap to solo habitation. Congratulations! (Make that a double mazel tov if you actually own the place.) Now, you might experience some jitters when living alone for the first time, ranging from paranoid (*Ohmygod, is that tap-tap-tapping outside my bedroom window the sound of raindrops or is it an ice-pick wielding serial killer who wants me to* think *it's the sound of raindrops*) to the morbidly curious (*If I choke to death on a pretzel, how long will it take before someone discovers my body?*). However, once the fear subsides and you get used to your own company, the benefits of living as a singular sensation far outweigh the 0.0000000000000001 percent chance that the tap-tap-tapping sound is, in fact, a serial killer with an ice pick. Plus, even though you probably won't ever Swiffer the kitchen floor while wearing only a headband and ankle socks, it's nice to know that you can do so without being judged for it by Kaitlyn, a twenty-one-year-old aspiring actress roommate you found on Craigslist to split the rent and the utilities.

LIVING LA VIDA ANIMAL HOUSE: Yaffa blocks? Check. (They're so convenient.) Three roommates? Check. (Always someone to watch *Iron Chef* with.) Beer pong table? Check. (Hey, it also doubles as a dining room table!) You loved college so much that you're still there in spirit. From house parties featuring flip-cup tournaments to a kitchen fully stocked with ramen noodles of every imaginable flavor, you're rocking the undergraduate lifestyle. As we've stressed many times before, there's no rulebook for how you should act post-quarter-life crisis. So, if you're happy displaying empty liquor bottles on your shelves, using tissues in place of napkins, and drip-drying rather than going out and buying more toilet paper, then that's all that matters. Oh, who are we kidding? Just like there comes a time when you have to bid farewell to sleeping until noon and wearing crop tops (actually, right now would be great), you'll also have to ditch that lame tapestry you bought at a Phish show (which you wore as a sarong and used as a blanket, table cloth, and curtains), eat off real plates, and cut back on watching the Food Network while taking bong hits with your roomies (okay, so maybe that last one can wait a bit longer).

COHABITATING AS A COUPLE: After months of schlepping an overnight bag back and forth between your boyfriend's apartment and yours (a.k.a. "the couples' commute"), you two crazy kids decide to move in together for all the right reasons (meaning it has absolutely nothing, we repeat *nothing*, to do with paying less money in rent). You can't wait to spend weekends strolling hand in hand through Pottery Barn in search of the perfect throw pillows for the new couch you picked up at West Elm. Sure, there will be a few sacrifices. For starters, you're going to have to get rid of the other man in your life, your beloved teddy bear, Buttons, since your boyfriend refuses to share the bed with a stuffed animal (even though Buttons has been in your life for almost two decades and deserves a more dignified send-off than being shoved into a closet). Then there's Mr. Perfect's gross habit of leaving his facial hair in the sink after shaving and his toenail clippings anywhere but the bathroom garbage can, not to mention how he uses condiments that expired six months ago and, oh, there's his minor porn addiction (if that last one hasn't come up yet, trust us, it will). Well, to be fair, you probably have some gross habits, too, like eating spoonfuls of Pillsbury Funfetti frosting out of the can, French kissing your Yorkie Poo, and squeezing your blackheads in the bathroom mirror. Oh, and we're pretty sure that even the most evolved male gets queasy around an economy-sized box of super-plus tampons. (Hell, even we do.) Here's the ugly truth about cohabitation: It doesn't guarantee happily ever after. About half of all couples that move in together end up separating within five years, according to the Centers for Disease Control. (By the way, shouldn't they be more concerned about swine flu outbreaks than breakups?) Still, if you can, in the words of Tim Gunn, "make it work," it can be rather fun waking up every morning with your boo and not worrying about accidentally walking in on your roommate and her boyfriend practicing positions from *The Cosmo Kama Sutra.*

MARTHA STEWART ON CRACK: A few years ago, you didn't own a full set of silverware—sorry, flatware—and you thought a sconce was something they served with tea and clotted cream in England. Then, something inside you snapped (perhaps due to insecurity, a growing obsession with shelter porn magazines, or an attempt to overcompensate for the lack of something or other in your life) and you became Martha Stewart on crack, the homemaker from hell. Now, let's get this straight. There's a big difference between having a flair for cooking, decorating, and entertaining (we love knitting and baking as much as the next girl, and we even give you some home ideas below, in "Experts Answer Your Most Burning Questions") and going all domestic *godless* when a dinner party guest accidentally spills a drop of Pinot Noir on your custom-upholstered suede loveseat that is most definitely *not* from IKEA. If your obsession with recreating the perfect home straight out of (what else?) *Martha Stewart Living* starts to affect your relationships with other people and overshadows the important things in life, it might be time to look beyond the hard-carved granite surface and get to the root of the problem. (Hint: It's a probably a mess that no amount of nontoxic, biodegradable, environmentally friendly, lavender-scented cleaning products will be able to kill.)

What's Really Going on When It Comes to Your Home Life: A Little Psychological Perspective

For Americans, home has always been more than where we lay our heads at night. It's a symbol of accomplishment, a dream realized, and, once we buy a house, tangible proof that we've come of age.

"A house symbolizes a whole new life," says our psychology tutor, Dr. Kevin Brennan. "It's the separation between young adult and adult."

During your early twenties, your home is incidental. It's a place to crash at night, a string of addresses as you move around in search of jobs, excitement, and yourself. As you get older, you want more than a roof over your head. Your home becomes a reflection of yourself, a haven from the outside world, and a place to lay down roots. "Eventually, we focus on what's there when we come home at night," says Dr. Kevin.

However, we're facing a couple of big problems when it comes to housing in our redo-berty years. From a practical perspective, real estate is way·more expensive that in was during our parents' generation. By one account, the amount of family income devoted to "fixed costs" such as housing, child care, health insurance, and taxes has gone from 53 to 75 percent in the past two decades. The other problem we're having with our home life has to do with our relentless pursuit of happiness and perfection—the need to have the biggest, baddest McMansion on the block.

"Home isn't just a place to live; it's an image," reiterates Dr. Kevin.

Oh, how HGTV has warped us all.

Adult Education: Experts Answer Your Most Burning Questions about Home, Entertaining, and Your Nest (Shudder)

It can happen while you're browsing through a glossy shelter magazine, visiting a friend at her swanky new digs, or after moving in with your significant other. The urge to become a domestic goddess and enter the world of 600-thread-count sheets, monogrammed wineglasses, and homemade loaves of pumpkin bread is a rite of passage into adulthood. That's why we consulted the experts for easy, budget-conscious ways to do everything from pulling off a killer party to "editing" your place (that's home decor speak for throwing out a lot of crap). So crack open a nice bottle of Shiraz and be blown away the brilliance of our hostesses with the mostesses: Katie Lee, author of *The Comfort Table*, and Erica Domesek, founder and author of the insanely cool DIY brand and book *P.S.- I made this* . . .

Burning Question #1: What are five things I should always have in my kitchen (and we're not talking about beer, beer, beer, champagne, and beer)?

Hey, we all like making reservations—and who hasn't developed a strong bond with their local Chinese takeout delivery guy?—but neither option is easy on your wallet (or your waistline). If you stock up on some culinary building blocks, cooking will become a more convenient and appealing option. Chef and entertainer extraordinaire Katie Lee suggests keeping the following versatile ingredients in your kitchen:

1. Fresh herbs: They make everything taste better. A couple of tablespoons can take your grilled chicken breast from blah to bravo.
2. Pasta: It's versatile and makes for a quick and inexpensive meal.
3. Cheeses: Keep a few different kinds, like a goat, cheddar, parmesan, and bleu. If friends drop by, you can put together a cheese plate in minutes. (Give yourself extra credit if you can say "cut the cheese" without giggling.)
4. Lemons: A squeeze of fresh lemon juice will brighten up any dish and add flavor. Lemon juice is also great for marinades, salad dressings, and cocktails.

5. Eggs: Scramble for breakfast, make a pasta carbonara, or whip up an omelette seasoned with fresh herbs (the ones you now have on hand) and a side salad for a simple dinner.

Burning Question #2: How can I entertain at my place without spending a lot of money or getting stuck in the kitchen?

Sure Tostitos are tasty (especially when paired with that so-gross-it's-good artificial cheese dip), but opening up a bag of chips—even the addictive Hint of Lime flavor—ain't gonna wow your guests. The key to throwing a successful and creative get-together is starting with a theme or general vision to facilitate the planning and keep your bash on track, says Erica Domesek, who came up with three fun and affordable party ideas. (By the way, much like you shouldn't watch *Top Chef* or go grocery shopping when you're hungry, you should probably have a snack before you read this list because it's going to make your stomach growl):

TUSCAN
Do you consider slice-and-bake cookies a challenge? Does your oven function as a storage device for your shoes? Is your freezer stocked with microwave meals? If you answered "yes" to any of the questions above, then this is the motif for you since it requires zero cooking.
DECOR: Stick tall thin candles in empty wine bottles and spark them up before your guests arrive so the wax has already begun to drip down. You can also repurpose wine corks for seating cards. Use an X-Acto knife to make one slit on the long round side a place a guest's name card in the slit. If you have a chalkboard, write a cute message or jot down your menu.
FOOD: For snacks, serve olives and nuts in rustic terra-cotta dishes (available at garden and hardware stores). For the main course, order in a bunch of pizzas from your local joint, preferably the brick-oven

thin-crust kind, which looks more homemade. Now here comes the fun part: Cut the slices into bite size squares and arrange them on a wood cutting board. Garnish individual pieces with fresh basil leaves, kalamata olives, sun-dried tomatoes, or whatever toppings you like. If the pizza has a crust, cut it into strips and serve alongside olive oil for dipping. You can also use a fork to crumble a block of parmesan cheese into a small dish and set out cups of olives.

DRINKS: Serve vino at dinner, but greet guests with glasses of Prosecco. It's an inexpensive Italian sparkling wine available at any liquor or wine store.

MOROCCAN
It's hard to invite your friends over for dinner if you don't have a proper dining table or enough chairs for everyone. This Arabian-inspired dinner party solves that problem while creating an intimate mood. (Make that *very* intimate if you can get your hands on a hookah.)

DECOR: Layer colorful scarves or old sarongs on the floor as your tablecloth and use pillows as your seats. For ambiance, use votive candles, incense, and brightly colored flowers in teacups.

FOOD: Doctor up your favorite store-bought boxed couscous with raisins, dried cranberries, pine nuts, and precooked grilled chicken strips. (Leave out that last one if any of your guests are vegetarians.) Now, separate a head of Boston lettuce, and arrange the leaves on a platter. These will be the wraps for the couscous. Serve with assorted chutneys and dipping sauces on a tray. (Unless you happen to be a whiz at making chutney, pick up a few options at the grocery store.)

DRINKS: Serve up wine in small juice glasses instead of traditional stemware.

BAGEL BAR AND BLOODY MARY BRUNCH
When you reach a certain age—and especially if you live in an urban

area—brunch, the decadent hybrid of breakfast and lunch, almost becomes a religion (mmm . . . pancakes). Yet what seems like a lovely idea inevitably becomes a huge letdown starting with the thirty-minute wait and ending with the bill ($13 for a watered-down mimosa?!). A better idea: Tell your crew to come to your place for some bagels and bloodies, no reservation required.

DRINKS: First, rim highball glasses (or regular water glasses) with Old Bay seasoning. Then, in a large pitcher combine Bloody Mary mix and vodka. (FYI: Serving mixed drinks in pitchers will make your alcohol last longer—plus people won't know if you used the cheap stuff.) Fill up bowls with tasty garnishes so your guests can personalize their potions (options: celery stalks, lemon wedges, lime wedges, green olives, several types of pickle options, hot and sweet peppers, and other picked items such as green beans and carrots) and don't forget Tabasco sauce and salt and pepper.

FOOD: Arrange a variety of pre-sliced bagels in a basket lined with a cloth napkin or kitchen hand towel. Set out a selection of "schmears" for the bagel bar ranging from the standards like butter and cream cheese (plain, veggie, chive, and whipped) to savory options like lox, capers, sliced onion, tomatoes, and cucumbers; store-bought tuna, chicken, and/or egg salad. You can also have some sweet spreads such as peanut butter, jams, Nutella, honey, sliced bananas, apples, and strawberries.

See, we told you that you were going to be hungry.

Burning Question #3: I'm moving in with my significant other. How can we merge our stuff together without killing each other?

Don't be freaked out if, when you first move in together, you two have a huge fight that will make you rethink your decision to cohabitate. The cause of the domestic altercation? He'll demand that you remove three-quarters of the pillows from the bed, and you'll threaten to put his collection of [insert name of favorite sports team here] bobble-heads on eBay. That's because merging really means purging, says Erica. "If you haven't worn a shirt, used a vase, or lit a scented candle in a year, give it the heave-ho." But before you start tossing out each other's crap with abandon, make sure you discuss what items you truly can't part with and try to figure out how to display them in a more appealing way. For example, those bobbleheads might not be so offensive if they were arranged on a shelf . . . a very, very high shelf in the linen closet.

Another helpful tip: Choose a color palette that you both love or at least can live with (blues, browns, or grays are all good, neutral options). This will make it easier to decide what items from your in-dividual homes will make the cut. "If you pick a palette that doesn't work with some of your furniture and accessories, you can always re-paint, reupholster, or buy slipcovers," says Erica, who also notes that it can be a bonding experience to take on a renovation project together, since nothing says "crazy in love" like a trip to Home Depot.

Lastly, don't worry if you live in an extremely small apartment or house. Sofas, tables, and art that you love but don't work in your cramped quarters can always go into a storage facility. Just because you can't find a place for them now doesn't mean that they won't be perfect when you move, redecorate, and upgrade. Kind of like your boyfriend.

Burning Question #4: How can I give my apartment a make-over without spending a lot of money?

Even if you have Pottery Barn taste on a Dollar Store budget, you can still revamp your pad with these five ingenious ideas from our doyenne of decor, Erica Domesek:

1. **Organize your bookshelves.** To create an artistic, gallery-like vibe, group your books by color and then arrange the hues (blues/greens, reds/pinks, whites, blacks/grays) on each shelf.

2. **Change your lampshades.** This one small detail can give any room a more put-together feel. Experiment with different shapes and bold colors like a black matte drum shade, which is bit masculine, or a colorful oversized one. You can find really cool options at Anthropologie or justshadesny.com.

3. **Raise the roof.** If you have average (i.e. low) ceilings, hanging your curtains higher up will make your room appear taller and create the illusion of larger windows. Here's how: Raise the rod above the window anywhere from a half a foot to a few inches from the ceiling, depending on what you're working with.

4. **Fake a headboard.** Who says that a grown-up has to have a headboard? You can make one for practically nothing. Paint a block of color the width of the bed with a unique shade that stands out from the rest of the walls in your bedroom. Then, place Euro-sized pillows behind standard ones. This adds height and depth to back of the bed and solves the sans-headboard issue altogether.

5. **Think outside the frame.** When it comes to wall space, you could go the standard route and hang framed paintings or prints, but there are other creative (and inexpensive) alternatives for giving your place some personal flair. Display decorative plates, antique flags or pennants, old tennis racquet, rowing oars, skis, etc. Or scour flea markets and eBay for cool vintage items.

Burning Question #5: Other than a bottle of wine or flowers, what's a good gift to bring when someone invites you to their house? We thought bringing some ShamWows was a great idea, but it didn't get the warm reception we thought it would at the last housewarming we attended. So we'll defer to Katie Lee, whose manners are just slightly better than ours. "I love to give homemade gifts because it shows that you put time and care into the gift, which is invaluable," she says. Her suggestions: Make a loaf of banana bread or whip up a batch of granola; then wrap it in clear plastic and tie with a beautiful ribbon. P.S. Don't tell Katie we said this, but if your baking skills are subpar, pick up an Entenmann's All Butter Loaf Cake, ditch the box, and pass that golden goodness off as homemade.

Quiz: Choose the Real IKEA Product

Ah, IKEA. Besides Alexander Skarsgård, it's our favorite Swedish import. The meatballs and lingonberry juice, the shopping cart full of things you never thought you'd need, and the exotic product names that have a shortage of vowels! In fact, here's a little quiz to see how well you know your stylish yet affordable self-assembled furniture, storage units, and other domestic doo-dads. Choose the real IKEA product from list of three names.

1. a. BJÖRN ULVAEUS
   b. BABYBJÖRN
   c. BEDDINGE

2. a. MY BOO
   b. MYSA LJUNG
   c. MAO ZEDONG

3. a. REXBO
   b. RAMBO
   c. RAINBOW

4. a. BIBY
   b. BUBBY
   c. BEBE

5. a. FJORD
   b. FLÄRKE
   c. FGRJHED

Answers

1. c: BEDDINGE is a sofa bed, perfect for your jobless deadbeat friends to crash on for weeks on end. (BJÖRN ULVAEUS is a former member of Swedish supergroup ABBA, and a BABYBJÖRN is a carrier you use to strap a child to your body.)

2. b: MYSA LJUNG is a toasty comforter. (Kelly Rowland sang about MY BOO in the hot Nelly jam "Dilemma," and MAO ZEDONG was the leader of the People's Republic of China from 1949 until 1976.)

3. a: Although it sounds like a type of illegal performance-enhancement drug that baseball players inject into their asses, REXBO is actually the name of an IKEA shelving unit. (RAMBO still kicks ass, even though he's a hundred years old, and RAINBOWS are so pretty.)

4. a: BIBY is a glass door cabinet that would probably elicit some color language from you if you attempt to assemble it. (Your BUBBY likes to kvetch, and BEBE makes clothes that you're getting too old to wear.)

5. b: FLÄRKE is a line of shelving units, perfect for organizing all of your useless shit that you probably should just throw out anyway. (A FJORD is a valley that was cut out by glaciers, and FGRJHED is the result of us, the authors, hitting random keys on the computer keyboard.)

IN CONCLUSION

The redo-berty years represent a time when you actually enjoy staying in and watching TV ("Honey, there's a new *Law & Order: SVU* on tonight!"). As a result, you start to take more of an interest in your home and entertaining. If there were an official checklist of things that make you an authentic adult, we're fairly certain that the desire to replace your cabinet hardware with chic new knobs or the ability to host a party that doesn't involve red plastic cups would be on it. But that doesn't mean you need to undergo an extreme home makeover. As our experts shared, there are tons of accessible, affordable ways to give your pad a fresh new look. Speaking of, we're assuming that after reading this chapter you'll want to start one of those inspiration boards with clips from decor magazines, fabric swatches, and photographs. So with that in mind, we thought it would be nice to contribute something. Here's a crib sheet of what you just read about for your laminating pleasure.

1. There's a difference between making a mean casserole and being a suburban psycho.
2. Real estate is way expensive.
3. Going out is fun, but at the end of the day, it's all about what you come home to.
4. Ordering in pizza can be considered "entertaining."
5. Nesting, nesting, nesting!

Flashback: The Tao of Judy Blume

While we love television and movies, nothing can capture the emotional roller coaster ride of adolescence like a good book. There were the riveting tales of preteen angst that kept you locked in your room, devouring each page until you found out what happened in the end; the juicy reads that got passed around your group of girlfriends; and the totally relatable characters that made you think that maybe somebody out there actually understands. These classics hold some serious girl wisdom that you can still use today.

THE BOOKS: The collected works of Judy Blume

A BRIEF REFRESHER: Just like we grouped all of John Hughes's movies together into one category in order to avoid writing an entire book about his insightful and endearing tales of teen angst, we're doing the same thing for Judy Blume, who gets mad props for penning enjoyable and realistic portrayals of girls struggling through the ups and downs of adolescence. Never one to talk down to her audience or tiptoe around tough subject matter, Judy Blume touches upon religion, periods, boys, and bras in *Are You There God? It's Me, Margaret* ("We must, we must, we must increase our bust!"); first sexual relationships in *Forever* (and as with *Flowers in the Attic*, which is summarized below, we know you flipped right to the good stuff in this book); masturbation in *Deenie*; and bullying and body image in *Blubber*. All in all, Judy Blume has written nearly thirty books, and she isn't stopping anytime soon. Plus, she has become a champion in the fight against censorship because plenty of old fuddy-duddies get their Victorian bloomers in a twist over the honesty in her pages. For this alone, we upgrade our previously mentioned "mad props," and give Judy Blume "stark-raving-angry props."

WHAT YOU CAN LEARN FROM THESE BOOKS TODAY: So much of what we read in these novels is still valid during our lives today. Mostly, keep in mind that it's not always easy being a girl (we mean *woman*), but we wouldn't give it up for anything in the world. And, it's nice to know that we aren't alone when it comes to things like body issues, boys, and just trying to find a place where we fit in.

THE BOOKS: The Baby-Sitters Club series

A BRIEF REFRESHER: The series that did for baby-sitting what *Twilight* did for drinking blood, the BSC books was about a group of friends living in the fictional town of Stoneybook, Connecticut, who form a club (can you guess the name?) that matches parents with adolescent child care specialists. The founding members include President Kristy Thomas, the bossy tomboy with a fondness for softball; Vice President Claudia Kishi, the artsy chick who has a private line in her room; Secretary Mary Anne Spier, the mousy good girl with a boyfriend (shout out to Logan Bruno!); and Treasurer Stacey McGill, the fashionista who has diabetes. (When business picks up, they eventually add two junior members and a few associates.) Throughout the series the girls experience everything from practical jokes (here's looking at you, Betsy Sobak) and questionable hair styles (cough, Stacey's perm, cough) to wicked stepsisters and tragic fashion choices (who can forget the insane descriptions of Claudia's outfits such as this gem: "baggy wool men's pants, gathered at the waist by a black leather band; a white tuxedo shirt with rolled-up sleeves; Capezio-type flats with mismatched white and black socks; and a glittery bow-tie barrette in her hair").

WHAT YOU CAN LEARN FROM THESE BOOKS TODAY: Parents will always be too ~~lazy~~ busy to watch their own children, making baby-sitting a lucrative career choice even if you're over the age of 16. But if watching other people's children isn't your thing, you can still take a page (maybe even literally) from this book and apply it to your life. If you're tired of the daily grind, why not start your own business?

THE BOOKS: The Sweet Valley High series

A BRIEF REFRESHER: The original chick lit series, the SVH books are about Elizabeth and Jessica Wakefield, identical sixteen-year-old twin sisters growing up in California. Within the first three pages of every book, you are reminded that the girls are way more gorgeous than you could ever be with their shoulder-length, sun-streaked blond hair, sparkling blue-green eyes, flawless tanned skin, adorable tiny dimples on their left cheeks, and perfect size-six figures. (And file this under our society's unhealthy obsession with being thin: In the recent up-dates to these books, the girls are now size fours.) But despite their carbon copy appearance, the sisters are *way* different. Elizabeth writes for the school paper, has a steady boyfriend, and *really, really* likes to read (SNOOZE). Jessica is the captain of the cheerleading squad. (Translation: the hobag.) Then there are the tertiary characters: Enid Rollins, Liz's geeky best friend (with that name did she even have a shot at coolness?); Lila Fowler, Jessica's rich-bitch frenemy (she drives a lime-green Triumph!); Bruce Patman, a precursor to Chuck Bass; Steven, the twins' smoking-hot brother; and Ned and Alice, their DILF and MILF parents. The Wakefield sisters experience everything from mundane teenage drama to over-the-top craziness (comas, kid-napping, plane crashes), but perhaps the most riveting aspect of the series is the cover art (we're talking about the originals, not the mod-ernized twenty-fifth anniversary versions where the girls look like characters from *The O.C.*). Our favorite: *The New Jessica* (SVH #32), where a khaki-pants-clad Elizabeth appears to be OMG-ing over Jessica's radical makeover.

WHAT YOU CAN LEARN FROM THESE BOOKS TODAY: Sorry, but these books are the least realistic of this whole list. In fact, if you ever see gorgeous teenage blond twins walking down the street, chances are they're on their way to the Playboy Mansion.

THE BOOK: *Go Ask Alice*

A BRIEF REFRESHER: Admit it—as you read this book, you felt like a total badass (and so retro, since it published in 1971). *Go Ask Alice* was heralded as the "real" diary of an average fifteen-year-old (but it was later revealed as a big fat fake) who goes from being an insecure loner whose biggest concern is her weight to kicking it with the cool crowd and dating a drug dealer. It all starts when Alice (what are we supposed to call her, "Anonymous"?) unknowingly drinks a Coca-Cola laced with LSD at a party (cue Jefferson Airplane). Acid must be one hell of a gateway drug, because before you can say "Just Say No," she's moved onto marijuana, amphetamines, and speed, which she lets her new friend Bill inject into her arm. After losing her virginity and having a pregnancy scare, Alice starts hanging out with a hippie chick named Chris, who introduces her to Richie. Soon Alice is selling drugs to grade-school kids to support him—that is until she catches her boyfriend in bed with another dude. AWKWARD. The rest of the book is a downward spiral of heroin, rape, and a stint in a mental hospital. Sadly, there's no happy ending for Alice since, according to the epilogue, she dies of an overdose.

WHAT YOU CAN LEARN FROM THIS BOOK TODAY: If you party like "Alice," it's time for rehab. Yes, indeed, drugs are really bad, but making up a bunch of stories about doing drugs is very lucrative. Even better? Try blogging about them.

THE BOOK: *Flowers in the Attic*

A BRIEF REFRESHER: Paging all you perverts! Don't deny that you skipped straight to all the dirty parts of V. C. Andrews's tawdry, twisted, and trashtastic tale of maternal abandonment, grandmotherly abuse, and brotherly and sisterly, um, biblical love. Christopher, Catherine, and the babies of the family, twins Cory and Carrie, have the perfect life (and all four of them possess the *Village of the Damned*–blond good looks that are so popular in these types of books). Actually, they *had* the perfect life—until their dad died in a car crash and left them penniless and heartbroken. After the accident, their mother, Corinne, does what any caring parent would do: She moves the whole family to the creepy mansion in Virginia where her evil yet filthy-rich parents reside, in the hopes that she can get back in their good graces (more on why she was in their bad graces in a bit) and earn a sizable inheritance once her father shuffles off to the creepy mansion in the sky (or, in his case, that mansion is probably located underground, right past the River Styx). Personally, we think it would have been easier to just get a job, but Corinne lacks any marketable skills, with the exception of her shiny blond hair. While her plan seems rather brilliant at first, there is a bit of a problem: In order to get her money, Corrine's first marriage wasn't supposed to have produced any children, which seems like an odd stipulation for a will, until she reveals to Christopher, Catherine, Cory, and Carrie that their father was actually her half uncle. Ewwww. Well, luckily for Corinne, that creepy old mansion has an attic, which provides the perfect place to hide away her demon-spawn children and make her father believe that she never procreated with drunk Uncle What's-His-Name. Fueled by greed, Corinne lets her sadistic mother whip, starve, berate, and imprison the *Village of the Damned* quartet, not to mention rob them of their youth, their health, and their will to live. Oh yeah—and Catherine and Christopher end up doing it. Like mother, like daughter. And like father/half great-uncle, like son.

WHAT YOU CAN LEARN FROM THIS BOOK TODAY: Let's keep this simple: Don't do anything that anyone does in this book. (And don't see the movie version of *Flowers in the Attic*, either. It stinks.) And, unfortunately, some family members are so psychotic (like the evil grandmother) that no matter how hard you try to forge a healthy relationship, nothing will help. Now that you're an adult, take refuge in the fact that some things are beyond your control. You owe it to yourself to steer clear of people who are harmful to your health.

THE BOOK: *Bridge to Terabithia*

A BRIEF REFRESHER: Like a nice long shower that washes away the filth of V. C. Andrews's "incest is best" tale, *Bridge to Terabithia* speaks of the strength of friendship, the power of imagination, and the pain of losing someone you love. Wouldn't it be great to have an escape hatch underneath your desk at work (and by escape hatch, we don't mean a bottle of booze) that transported you to a happy place whenever the going got tough? Well, unlikely best friends fifth graders Jesse (a star runner from a not-so-great family who is afraid to let his classmates and father know about his artistic aspirations) and Leslie, (a tomboy who could give a rat's ass how other people view her) have the ultimate escape hatch: a rope swing that transports them across the creek to the make-believe kingdom of Terabithia. Here, in their happy place, they rule as king and queen and forget about the general shittiness of puberty. As their friendship strengthens, so do their identities—until the ultimate tearjerker. One day, Jesse goes away on a school trip and comes back to discover that Leslie drowned in the creek as she tried to go to Teribithia without him. (How's that for a downer?) After grieving, he ultimately realizes that the memory of her will live on.

WHAT YOU CAN LEARN FROM THIS BOOK TODAY: Never underestimate the power of friendship, especially one that, on the surface, seems like an unlikely pairing. Hell, maybe you can actually learn from each other. And, don't ever swing on a rope unattended. (We can't believe we just made a joke about this book because it did really make us cry when we read it.)

Part III

Bonus Features: You're All Grows Up, So Deal with It

This is the section of the book where we teach you how to cope with any anxiety you feel about getting older and also give some more concrete advice. Think of it as the DVD bonus material.

Eleven

Mind Your Manners:
Grown-up Etiquette Queries and Quandaries

A girl should be two things: classy and fabulous.

—Coco Chanel

I don't want to pierce anything. I think it's outdated. Belly rings and all are, like, old.

—Britney Spears

YOU'RE AN adult now, which means that you should at least attempt to exude grace, dignity, and maturity. We know, easier said than done, especially during a time when no one wants to keep private matters out of the public eye or learn how to exit a car without flashing her privates. (Hint: Wearing underwear helps.) In order to guide you on your journey to real womanhood, we've rounded up a group of experts to give advice—in their own words—for some tricky issues and sticky situations that you might be dealing with right now.

HERE COMES THE DRAMA: WED-IQUETTE

The redo-berty years will suck you into a vortex of vows. Sure, weddings are fun, but the sheer number during your late twenties and early thirties can leave you exhausted, hung over, and thin in the bank account. However, according to our experts, Erin Torneo and Valerie Cabrera Krause, coauthors of *The Bridal Wave: A Survival*

Guide to the Everyone-I-Know-Is-Getting-Married Years, there are ways to make closets full of hideous bridesmaids dresses, piles of penis paraphernalia, and numerous awful wedding band renditions of "Livin' on a Prayer" slightly less painful. (And they're not talking about hitting the open bar like drunken Uncle Lou.)

I agreed to be in a wedding, but due to some recent financial setbacks, I can no longer afford to pay for everything. Is it okay to pull out?

FROM ERIN AND VALERIE: Chances are that the bride asked you to be a part of her wedding party because she sees you as a very close friend. If she is still a rational person and not yet *lobridemized*, tell her that you have had some hard times and will be unable to fulfill your bridesmaid duties but you are honored that she asked and you definitely want to help her in other ways. Volunteer to run wedding errands with her. Look at dresses and attend practice makeup and hairdo sessions—these sorts of things won't cost you anything but time. But make sure she doesn't catch you rocking brand-new $500 boots. True financial hardship is a valid excuse. If you are more of an "I have the money but don't want to spend it on another crappy dress and shower hosting expenses girl," come up with another (better) excuse.

My friends are getting married left and right and I'm beyond single. How can I be happy for them without secretly feeling bitter?

FROM ERIN AND VALERIE: That is the million-dollar question. It's natural to feel envious and wonder if your life isn't tracking. The key is to not allow it to drag you under. You cannot control when you fall in love, so focus on what you can control in your life. Hate your job? Take steps to find a new career. Feeling flabby? Sign up for a 10K and get running. And if you are in a dating drought, ask your newlywed friends to set you up!

Can I request that my significant other is invited since we've been together longer than many of the married friends who are going to be in attendance? Is that really rude?

FROM ERIN AND VALERIE: Hmmm. That depends. Does the betrothed know your boyfriend? Is the wedding super small? If the wedding is tiny and they don't know your beau, suck it up and go it alone. If they know him and/or it's not a small wedding, ask. If you are told that you cannot bring a plus one, be gracious and then decide whether it's enough of an issue for you to send your regrets and miss the shindig.

All of my friends are getting married. Do I have to give an engagement, shower, and wedding gift? And what about anniversaries? Please say I don't need to buy them a gift for those, too.

FROM ERIN AND VALERIE: No engagement gift necessary. If you are inclined, a card is a lovely gesture. The main thing is to just act really excited and interested in the engagement story. If you attend the shower, you'll need to give a gift, but you don't have to if you're not attending. And really? The wedding gift? You are pretty much signed up to give one as soon as your name goes on the invite list, whether or not you attend. As for the anniversary gift, you're off the hook. Valerie got an anniversary card from a friend and thought it was nice but kind of weird.

BABY MAMA DRAMA: CHILDISH MATTERS

First comes love; then comes marriage; then comes a real, live human being that demands undivided attention in a baby carriage. Let's face it: Babies are cute (well, most of them, anyway), but they have an uncanny knack for testing friendships. New parents become obsessed with their new little angel's every bowel movement, while the child-less wonder what the hell a Boppy is (for the record, it's a special pillow that's supposed to enhance bonding time between Mommy and Baby). Meredith Levy, founder and publisher of the online magazine *Pint Size Social*, has advice for both sides.

My best friend had a baby a few months ago, and while I knew things would be different, I didn't expect it to be so hard to relate to her. What can I do to keep our friendship alive?

FROM MEREDITH: Try to understand that what she is going through is most likely throwing off her life much more than it is yours (Authors' note: The woman just pushed a baby out of her hoo-ha, for crying out loud), so it's really up to you to be proactive about the friendship. Most new moms are completely exhausted in the beginning, but after the first three months, your friend's life will start to normalize, only now she has a baby. And while she may not be in the mood for late nights out, she will definitely want to hang out with you, so remember the things you loved doing together that don't revolve around bars and drinking, like going shopping, watching movies, getting manicures, etc.

I recently had a baby, and after visiting me once or twice, my childless friends seem to have totally forgotten about me. They just aren't inviting me out like they used to. I know they probably assume that I'm busy with the baby, but I feel really left out. Any advice?

FROM MEREDITH: They are thinking two things: one, that you are crazy busy, and two, that you have no time for them. The best thing you can do to maintain your sanity (and your husband's, for that matter) is to schedule some "me time," which includes seeing your friends. And, while their late-night single life may not be as appealing to you right now, try to do things that you loved doing together in daylight hours. Hire a baby-sitter and make an effort. The worst thing is to wake up a year after you had your baby and realize you have alienated your friends. And, do not talk about your baby the entire time. Show one or two pictures, and show interest in their lives. It will take your mind off of your life and give you a much-needed break from changing diapers and night feedings.

If I invite people with children to a dinner party, is there a polite way to tell them to leave their kids at home?

FROM MEREDITH: When you send out the invitation, make it very clear who is and isn't invited. The best way to do this without pissing off anyone is to include a clever one-liner about how this is an adult party, no kids allowed. (Authors' recommendation: "Just a heads up, our dog Noodles, loves to eat children.") Any parent should get the hint.

How can I politely tell my mother-in-law to keep her unsolicited parenting advice to herself?

FROM MEREDITH: The most important thing to remember is that as annoying as her meddling may be, she is coming from a place of love and may not realize that her well-meaning suggestions actually feel like blistering criticisms of your parenting skills. The next time she starts a sentence with "It might help if you . . ." or "Back in my day we . . ." say "Thank you" and then ignore her. That said, before you totally tune her out, keep in mind that your mother-in-law has done this before (with the man you love, your husband) and might actually know a thing or two.

ONLINE OFFENSES: DIGITAL DRAMA

By now, you know it's really uncool to forward your friends chain letters that promise good fortune, but in this ever-changing era of social networking, there's a constant need for new rules and regulations. Mariann Hardey, Ph.D., the self-proclaimed "doyenne of digital etiquette," tells you how to handle the latest techno-trouble and not become one of *those* people. (You know who we're talking about: the iPhone addict who interrupts a conversation to show you that she just downloaded an app that lets her see if there are any sex offenders living in the area. Yes, there really is an app for that.)

Is it ever OK to defriend someone on Facebook?

FROM DR. HARDEY: Have they poked you in a delicate place? Then, yes, a defriending is in order. Defriending happens for a number of reasons, the most common being that said friend assaults you with mind-numbing updates. A word of caution, though: If you choose to defriend someone, you should also block them altogether as they may be offended by your actions and choose to write some very creative messages on your wall. However, if the friend in question is an ex, you want to retain some level of snooper-ship and thus, I would recommend that you do not defriend. Simply choose to observe from afar, which is not stalker behavior, but a necessary social survival tactic.

The girl who bullied me in high school requested my friendship on Facebook. Do I ignore her, accept her friendship, or confront her? Why would she try to find me again? They say time heals all wounds, but I'm still bitter that she called me a witch with a capital B back in the day.

FROM DR. HARDEY: So the witch is back to assert her power over you. She may have conveniently forgotten all about her dabble in the black arts of bullying during high school, and your teenage years were filled with enough trouble and angst without having to navigate around her actions. With a friend request, there is no context of where her actions are coming from. One possible scenario is that she has amended her ways and is a nicer and more rounded person. Another scenario (which could delight your curiosity) is that she is more rounded—all over. So you may take pleasure from finding out whether she matches her witch status on her outside as much as she did on her inside. Why has she tried to find you? Because she is "so sorry" and wants to grovel at your feet? Unlikely, but you could always click "Accept" and find out.

How do I deal when coworkers or, even worse, my boss or direct reports request my friendship on Facebook?

FROM DR. HARDEY: Friend them. You would not be a "co"-worker if you choose to ignore such requests. However, make sure that all such acquaintances have limited access to your profile and photos. After all, you would not open your entire life up to your boss, especially with regard to those late-night status updates.

When is it acceptable to text message/BlackBerry in public, and when should you power down?

FROM DR. HARDEY: Oh, you should always text and BlackBerry in public. If you don't, the person next to you will. If they are not texting right this minute, you can bet that they are thinking about it. You should only power down if there's been a nuclear disaster and you need to retain battery for emergency communication with Jack Bauer to come save you. (Authors' note: In case you were too busy texting to notice, Dr. Hardey is *kidding*.)

ADULT SITUATIONS: RANDOM RULES

Wondering if it's still OK to don short shorts or how to deflect unwanted inquiries about your personal life? These are just some of the miscellaneous predicaments that arise when you embark on your journey to becoming a real-deal adult. Jordan Christy, author *How to Be a Hepburn in a Hilton World: The Art of Living with Style, Class, and Grace*, shares her tips for looking, talking, and generally acting like a lady.

Am I ever too old to wear any particular article of clothing? (Women's magazines seem to think so, but I don't know if I completely buy that. . . .)

FROM JORDAN: As long as you're alive and breathing, you're never too old to wear particular articles of clothing. However, whether or not those articles of clothing look good on you is a whole other story. Ankle booties might be the hottest thing right now, but they usually only flatter those who weigh under ninety pounds or walk the runway for a living. Animal prints may also be back in a big way, but for someone over thirty-five, they tend to scream "trashy" rather than "sassy." In general, stay away from anything that sparkles, flashes, or resembles fish scales, and you'll be just fine.

How should I greet people the first time I meet them? A handshake seems kind of formal, and a hug feels very intimate. And at what point should I be kissing people on the cheek? What about guys?

FROM JORDAN: When greeting another lady: During an initial meeting, a handshake is completely appropriate. When paired with a sincere smile and engaging conversation, the handshake isn't at all too formal. After you've spent several minutes (or hours, depending on the circumstances) with the person in question, a kiss on the cheek is usually an acceptable and appropriate farewell. However, if you're meeting someone for the first time in person that you've had prior contact with (via email, phone, etc.), a hug is usually a warm and welcome greeting.

When greeting a guy: During an initial meeting (and farewell, for that matter), a handshake is always tactful and demure. A hug should be reserved for men whom you know well in the right setting. For example, you don't want to be reaching up and around for a six-foot bear hug in your diamond-encrusted, floor-length gown during the gala ball. And when it comes to a peck on the cheek, I'm of the mindset that if anyone's going to be doing any kissing, it's going to be the guy!

I'm single/in a relationship/married. How do I tactfully deal with people who don't know me asking personal questions like why don't you have a boyfriend?/when are you two getting married?/when are you having kids?

FROM JORDAN: It wouldn't be inappropriate to turn the (rude) inquiry into a joke and simultaneously turn the question back on them. For example:

1. Why don't you have a boyfriend? "Well, I have very high standards when it comes to guys. Do you happen to know anyone who has a six-figure income and looks like Brad Pitt?"
2. Why aren't you two married yet? "We're waiting out for the government to issue a stimulus package for honeymoons to Bora Bora. Have you ever been there?"
3. When are you having kids? "We haven't even figured out how to work the thermostat in our house yet, so we're holding out on raising a human being. You just moved into a new house, too, right?"

I just celebrated my thirtieth birthday, and a bunch of my friends chipped in on a nice gift. Do I have to write each of them a thank-you note, or is a mass email acceptable?

FROM JORDAN: I actually had a baby shower gift that fourteen people chipped in on. I spent the next three evenings on the floor next to my stationery box but, in the end, felt good that they each received a proper thank you. Anything less looks cheap. No matter the number of people, they each need a handwritten thank-you note.

Interesting Conversation Starters
When You're Stuck at the Singles' Table

Ah, weddings. A time for love, celebration, questionable etiquette, and traditions, like something borrowed, something blue, drunken Uncle Lou—and let's not forget the singles' table, the seating area that unintentionally ostracizes the unattached. (Think of it as one step above the card table that your mother used to set up in the kitchen for Thanksgiving dinner when there were too many grown-ups in the dining room.) Sure, the singles' table can be a lot of fun, but the next time you find yourself at a wedding reception and at a loss for words among a group of unattached strangers, here are some conversation starters that will definitely liven things up. Remember: Making excellent conversation is the polite thing to do.

1. I'd kill for a baby right now. No, really, *kill*. With my bare hands.
2. Do you ever hurt yourself to see if you still feel? Um, me neither.
3. You should read my *Twilight* fan fiction.
4. I was browsing the "Casual Encounters" section of Craigslist the other day . . .
5. Birth control is a pseudoscience.
6. So, how much money do you make?
7. I see dead people.
8. What would Xenu do?
9. It's like my shaman always says . . .

10. You're only as married as you feel.
11. Does anyone know if white wine gets out blood stains? My, um, friend really wants to know.
12. I'm only one surgery away from becoming a woman.
13. Remember the woman who was selling a sandwich with Jesus's face on eBay? That was me!

Sounding Off

According to our totally unscientific survey of real women, the older you get, the younger you feel. One possible explanation for this phenomenon? How about the fact that books about preteen wizards and teenage vampire-bait aren't just for kids anymore! We asked the women a tough question: **How old do you feel?**

"Sixteen. Sometimes when I buy liquor, I get nervous that they will bust me for being underage. Then I realize that I'm twenty-nine."—*Brooke, 29*

"Old enough to wear makeup semi-regularly and worry about savings, but not old enough for Botox and a mortgage."—*Jen, 26*

"I've always felt like an old soul. I reckon I'm about 132 years old."—*Carla, 27*

"It depends. I have the confidence and the knowledge of someone my age but I still can play and have fun like a twenty-five-year-old. I am half woman, half young adult, and probably will always be that way!"—*Laura, 32.5*

"While at work: forty-five. Outside of work with my friends: twenty-three. With my man: eighteen."—*Alix, 28*

"Twenty-six, tops."—*Julie, 29*

"Honestly, it depends on the day. There are days I feel like I'm twenty-one, there are days when I feel my age, and there are moments (not days) when I feel like I'm forty-five. But most days I feel like thirty-two, thrilled with where I am and where I'm headed."
—*Lis, 32*

"It depends on the day. Some days I feel eighteen, mostly because I am not entirely sure what happened to the past twelve years, and some days I feel twenty-eight. I don't think I've actually 'felt' thirty years old yet, but it's only been about six months, so we'll see."—*Melissa, 30*

"Somewhere between twenty-five and thirty—I think closer to thirty, but shhhhhhhh!"—*Lori, 30*

"Most days I feel like I'm nineteen—that magical age where you're over eighteen for real but you're young enough to still not have any real responsibilities."—*Danielle, 26*

"I still feel like I'm in my twenties. I can still party with the best of them and maybe sometimes even party harder than a twenty-year-old! It's all those years of practice!"—*Candice, 31*

Twelve

Kicking the Bucket List: Managing Your Life Goals

RELIGIOUS VIEWS aside, it's pretty likely that we only make one quick trip around this carousel of life before the music stops, the carnies kick us off, and a new group of kiddies gets to climb up onto the horsies for their chance to have all the fun. And, since time goes by quickly, it's important to have goals, whether they're daily tasks scribbled on a Post-it note or hopes and dreams hidden away in a journal.

Enter the bucket list, a concept sharing the same name as a movie that grossed boatloads of box-office dollars despite its high degree of shittiness. Even Jack Nicholson and Morgan Freeman couldn't save that stinking ship. Anyway, if you're not familiar with a bucket list, here's the deal: It's a lofty to-do list, a bunch of wonderful, exciting things that you're supposed to try before you die.

As if we don't already have enough pressure. As women, we're supposed to be career-driven yet maternal, domestic yet titillating, nice yet naughty, and perfect-looking yet low-maintenance. What else do they want from us?

How about, who cares? Seriously. If you create a bucket list, do it right. Rather than getting all Tracy Flick and moving from one checked-off box to another, fill the list with things you want to do, not what you *think* people should do. And, don't forget to include the really important stuff: Be yourself. Spend time with your loved ones.

Laugh a lot. Treat others the way you want to be treated. Get yourself onto the competitive eating circuit.

Now, let's take some of the heat off of you and expose some lofty life goals for what they really are.

SOME LOFTY LIFE GOALS AND WHY YOU SHOULDN'T FEEL GUILTY IF YOU DON'T SCRATCH THEM OFF YOUR BUCKET LIST

THE GOAL: Climb a really, really high mountain.

WHY IT'S OVERRATED: Two symptoms of severe high altitude sickness include swelling of the brain and frothy pink sputum. Eww.

INSTEAD, WHY DON'T YOU: Add "Read *Into Thin Air*" to your bucket list. Once you finish Jon Krakauer's terrifying and true account of a horrible tragedy on Mount Everest, you'll be replacing "climb a mountain" with "learn to salsa." If you still want to get your fix of pristine nature, watch the amazing *Planet Earth* series. (A word of advice: *Planet Earth* is doubly amazing if you watch it after drinking a little too much the night before. It's like the fountain of youth— but for hangovers! Perhaps David Attenborough's calm narration has magical healing powers.)

THE GOAL: Go skydiving.

WHY IT'S OVERRATED: Sure, jumping out of plane from ten thousand feet in the air sounds dangerous, but it's not as dangerous as you might think. Approximately 1 person dies per 100,000 jumps. Plus, getting strapped to a stranger while you go down sounds like something out of an episode of *Real Sex* on HBO.

THE ALTERNATIVE: Hey, Evel Knievel, why don't you get really crazy and drive your car somewhere! In fact, if you drive at least ten thousand miles per year, you would have to jump out of a plane about seventeen times (while wearing a parachute, of course) in order to match your risk of dying in a automobile, or so says the Naval Safety Center.

THE GOAL: Run with the bulls in Pamplona.
WHY IT'S OVERRATED: Because it's really, really stupid. (Sorry, boys—or sorry, the one boy who picked up this book—but there's a reason why women stay away from this festival: because we're smart.) Seriously, anyone who willingly gets that close to a gaggle of wild beasts deserves to get gored up the bum-bum.
INSTEAD, WHY DON'T YOU: Join a group of friends who are on the prowl. Around closing time at your local meat market, you'll feel an adrenaline rush as you try to escape another very different, yet equally wily, group of horny animals.

THE GOAL: Write a book.
WHY IT'S OVERRATED: Just trust us on this one, dear reader. We mean—it's great! A real dream come true!
INSTEAD, WHY DON'T YOU: Seek fame and fortune by creating a really clever iPhone app or a stupid as-seen-on-TV gadget that will sell like hotcakes. (Or, perhaps you can kill two birds with one stone and create an app that transforms your iPhone into a Ped Egg. And perhaps we can use another cliché because they make writing as easy as pie. There! That was a piece of cake! Anyway . . .)

THE GOAL: Lose a certain number of pounds that you think are standing in the way of happiness.
WHY IT'S OVERRATED: Stop beating yourself up about your weight.
INSTEAD WHY DON'T YOU: Take up boxing and fuel your workout by taking imaginary jabs and uppercuts at Hollywood and the fashion industry for trying to convince us that beauty only comes in one size: hungry.

THE GOAL: Literally have sex on the beach.

WHY IT'S OVERRATED: So we're guessing that you've never gotten sand stuck in the bottom of your bathing suit?

INSTEAD, WHY DON'T YOU: Have sex in a really, really nice hotel room overlooking the beach, where you'll be far from natural exfoliants that can, um, exfoliate stuff that shouldn't be exfoliated. (Like your privates.)

THE GOAL: Save the world.

WHY IT'S OVERRATED: This goal isn't so much overrated as it is unfocused. Hey, we can't hate on anyone who wants to do good deeds.

INSTEAD, WHY DON'T YOU: Think small for big results. Also, remember that true charity starts at home, and by that, we don't mean that you should treat yourself to that really expensive pair of shoes you've been ogling.

THE GOAL: Make a million bucks.

WHY IT'S OVERRATED: Don't you know anything about inflation or saving for retirement? In twenty years, dinner and a movie for two is going to cost about $1.2 million, and *Paul Blart: Mall Cop, Part 21* will gross more than $500,000,000,000,000,000,000,000 at the box office.

INSTEAD, WHY DON'T YOU: Get to work on that iPhone app that can smooth away a billion foot calluses and, hopefully, make you billions of dollars.

THE GOAL: Be in two places at once. (Yep, we totally ripped this one off from *A Walk to Remember*.)

WHY IT'S OVERRATED: We love, love, love Mandy Moore, but this movie is a bit much for our liking. (OK—stepping out of character for a moment—Andrea totally cried when she was watching it.)

INSTEAD WHY DON'T YOU: Watch *Saved!*

Sounding Off

As authors and your trusty guides through the redo-berty years, we couldn't resist getting in on the fun, too. . . .

What's the best part about being in your late twenties/early thirties?

"I used to worry that if I didn't have plans, especially on the week-ends, I was a total loser. But now I'm happy spending a Saturday night doing nothing. Sure, it could be because I'm getting older and going to the hot new club doesn't have the same appeal it once did, but I like to think it's more about being secure with who I am. That, and my DVR fills up really quickly during the week."—*Andrea, 30*

"I like having more self-confidence. There's no longer that burn-ing need to try out different identities and personas. I know who I am now, and I make no excuses for it. OK, correction: I make *fewer* excuses for it. Seriously, whenever a particularly embarrass-ing song pops up in rotation on my iPod, I've stopped turning the volume down out of fear that someone in the vicinity will know I'm rocking out to Rush."—*Jessica, 30*

What's the worst part about being in your late twenties/early thirties?

"Feeling like the decisions that I make right now are permanent and that I'm running out of time to accomplish some of the things on my life's to-do list. There's also an immense anxiety about my parents getting older. But what really sucks is the face people who are twenty-five and under make when I tell them that I'm thirty.

It's equal parts pity and fear. I want to tell them that, yes, it's contagious and before they know it, they'll be 'old,' too."—*Andrea*

"Age really is only a number, but let's be realistic: It's hard not to look around at what your peer group has accomplished personally and professionally and think, 'Uh-oh. Am I doing something wrong here?' On a superficial note, my metabolism finally rebelled, getting all up in my face, *Jerry Springer*–style, and shouting, 'Aw, hell no!' I had to kick my late-night diner habit, which hurt me right to my soul. Seriously, why can't the people who make Nicorette develop a patch that delivers the sheer delight of fries smothered with gravy right into your bloodstream?"—*Jessica*

Was there a particular moment in your life when you realized, "Holy shit, I'm officially an adult!"?

"When Jessica (as in my lovely coauthor) and I were invited to speak at our alma mater so the students could ask us career advice. There was also the moment when I was standing in my best friend's childhood bedroom holding her baby for the first time. That was pretty crazy."—*Andrea*

"I started to get interested in the stock market. Of course, true to the contradictory nature of the redo-berty years, I didn't actually have any money to invest in it."—*Jessica*

What did you think you'd be doing at this age?

"In fifth grade, my teacher told us to write an essay about what we wanted to be when we grew up. I must've been the most overly confident (or delusional) eleven-year-old because I wrote about becoming a supermodel. While my career choice was laughable, I guess the actual writing was decent because my teacher encouraged me to pursue creative writing. That, combined with an obsession with my mother's copies of *Ladies' Home Journal*, made me want to become a magazine editor. Career aspirations aside, what I really thought I'd be by now is a wife and mom."—*Andrea*

"When I was little, I thought I would grow up to be a mall Easter Bunny or a performer in the Ice Capades. As I got a little older, I went through a phase where I wanted to be a veterinarian, a career aspiration I abandoned as soon as I learned that my brother's friend, a vet school student, had to go elbow-deep into a cow in order to artificially inseminate her. Since I decided that the color of my parachute did not include cow spooge, I moved on to dreams of a far less 'icky' occupation: writer."—*Jessica*

How old do you feel?

"About twenty-five—until I have to leave a bar because it's too crowded, too loud, or filled with too many actual twenty-five-year-olds."—*Andrea*

"Most days, I feel like I'm twenty-five. However, on those mornings when I'm nursing a hangover, I feel about as old as Yoda, but without all of the wisdom."—*Jessica*

Conclusion

Growing Pains Don't Have to Actually Hurt: Why You Couldn't Pay Us to Be Twenty Again

I want to be thirty, flirty, and thriving.

—from *13 Going on 30*

TREES DO IT. Bees do it. Cats do it, and bats do it. Cher does it, and Hayden *Pantyhairs* does it. It doesn't matter if you're filthy rich or dirt poor, famous or anonymous, powerful or powerless. You're aging—hell, we're all getting older—even as you read these words. And, guess what? Just like puberty, it's only natural!

It's also only natural if you feel a little anxious about the escalating number of candles on your birthday cake. They're a reminder that you're human and mortal and have feelings—you know, the sort of deep stuff that Oprah likes to talk about. Our advice? Allow yourself a prescribed amount of time to worry about irrational things like dying alone—for example, how about getting all weepy during a *Project Runway* commercial break?—and then, let them go and live your life—not just a so-called one. Because here's the thing: Redo-berty can be turbulent, tumultuous, confusing, depressing, awful—insert any other scary adjectives here. However, they can also be exhilarating, exciting, fun, happy, and fulfilling. Even better, now is the time when you can have the best of both worlds: the energy of relative youth and the good sense that comes with adulthood. You're actually a lot like Jem, who was a sensible businesswoman by day (running

Starlight Music was no easy task), but at night (and with some assistance from her trusty computer Synergy), she transformed into a bad-ass chick who rocked out with the Holograms.

Sure, having the ability to travel between two worlds doesn't change the fact that you're no longer twenty years old. But, there's some good news: You're no longer twenty years old. Now, before you start waxing nostalgic about your ramen noodle years, let's take a look at your life today and what you've gained.

1. So, you might not be able to boot and rally anymore (we know, it's such an important skill), but you can buy those boots that you've been ogling without worrying about getting into trouble with your parents.

2. So, you might freak out after peeing on a stick and seeing two pink lines, but this time, you could very well be crying tears of joy.

3. You might still have cravings for unnecessary drama, but now it's a part of your must-see "reality" TV rather than the reality of your life.

4. You might still be looking for Mr. Right, but you've learned how to avoid Mr. Wrong (well, at least most of the time).

5. You might not have the job of your dreams, but you have an intern, which is pretty freaking cool.

6. You might not be able to pull off wearing a tube top, but you finally have the good sense to realize that no one can or should at any age.

7. You might not be able to sleep until noon, but you've actually learned to enjoy keeping hours fit more for a human being than a vampire.

8. You might be a mom, but you're a hot mom. (Just don't wear a rhinestone-encrusted tee that proclaims this.)

9. You might still care a lot about what other people think, only now, it's the people you care the most about.

10. You might not be rich and famous, but you're loved, and isn't that what really matters? Now, bring your old ass over here for a big group hug!

Essential Reading

Precious Resources to Further Your Adult Education

Below, we've listed some invaluable resources that can help you cope with all aspects of life in the redo-berty years.

BOOKS

Career and Finance

Brazen Careerist: The New Rules For Success, by Penelope Trunk (Business Plus, 2007)

How'd You Score That Gig?: A Guide to the Coolest Jobs (and How to Get Them), by Alexandra Levit (Ballantine Books, 2008)

New Job, New You: A Guide to Reinventing Yourself in a Bright New Career, by Alexandra Levit (Ballantine Books, 2009)

You're So Money: Live Rich Even When You're Not, by Farnoosh Torabi (Three Rivers Press, 2008)

Dating, Relationships, and Love

The Bridal Wave: A Survival Guide to the Everyone-I-Know-Is-Getting-Married Years, by Erin Torneo and Valerie Cabrera Krause (Villard, 2007)

His Cold Feet: A Guide for the Woman Who Wants to Tie the Knot With the Guy Who Wants to Talk About It Later, by Andrea Passman Candell (St. Martin's Griffin, 2008)

The Joy of Text: Mating, Dating, and Techno-Relating, by Kristina Grish (Simon Spotlight Entertainment, 2006)

Why He Didn't Call You Back: 1,000 Guys Reveal What They Really Thought About You After Your Date, by Rachel Greenwald (Crown, 2009)

Etiquette

How to Be a Hepburn in a Hilton World: The Art of Living with Style, Class, and Grace, by Jordan Christy (Center Street, 2009)

Family

The A to Z Guide to Raising Happy Confident Kids, by Dr. Jenn Berman (New World Library, 2007) (Dr. Berman also has a line of T-shirts called Retail Therapy.)

Walking on Eggshells: Navigating the Delicate Relationship Between Adult Children and Parents, by Jane Isay (Anchor, 2008)

Friendship

Best Friends Forever: Surviving a Breakup with Your Best Friend, by Irene S. Levine, Ph.D. (Overlook Press, 2009)

Friend or Frenemy?: A Guide to the Friends You Need and the Ones You Don't, by Andrea Lavinthal and Jessica Rozler, (Harper Paperbacks, 2008)

Health and Wellness

Because It Feels Good: A Woman's Guide to Sexual Pleasure and Satisfaction, by Debby Herbenick, Ph.D., MPH (Rodale Books, 2009)

The New Mom's Survival Guide: How to Reclaim Your Body, Your

Health, Your Sanity, and Your Sex Life After Having a Baby, by Jennifer Wider, M.D. (Bantam, 2008)

Home, Entertaining, and Hobbies

The Comfort Table: Recipes for Everyday Occasions, by Katie Lee (Simon Spotlight Entertainment, 2008)

Get a Hobby!: 101 All-Consuming Diversions for Any Lifestyle, by Tina Barseghian (Collins, 2007)

P.S.- I made this. . . : I See It. I Like It. I Make It., by Erica Domesek (Abrams Image, 2010)

WEBSITES AND BLOGS

Dr. Kevin, Psychologist for Young Professionals (www.DrKevinNYC.com—includes a great blog geared toward young professionals)

The Jet Set Girls (thejetsetgirls.blogspot.com)

Penelope Trunk's Brazen Careerist (blog.penelopetrunk.com)

Pint Size Social (www.pintsizesocial.com)

Practising a Proper Social Demeanour: A Guide to Facebook Etiquette (properfacebooketiquette.blogspot.com)

P.S.- I made this . . . (psimadethis.com)

Acknowledgments

We would be remiss (and frankly kind of rude) if we didn't thank all of the people who made *Your So-Called Life* possible, starting with the entire team at HarperCollins, including Jeanette Perez, our outstanding editor; Carrie Kania, for giving the book the green light and always supporting us; Audrey Harris, Alberto Rojas, and Vanessa Schneider, our publicists; Erica Weinberg, our wonderful production editor; Mary Beth Constant, the copyeditor who made us laugh with her hilarious comments; and Robin Bilardello for the cover (we love it!).

Much gratitude to all of the wonderful experts who offered their advice to this book. You're the greatest.

Obviously we want to give double air-kisses to our brilliant and supportive agent, Adam Chromy of Artists and Artisans Inc. Once again you helped us turn an idea into a book (and not one with "Puberty" in the title). You're the best and we adore you.

We also want to thank our parents for not screwing us up, and our big brothers for not causing permanent damage from years of headlocks.

And, last, but never ever least, cheers to all of our amazing friends. You are the reason we write these books and we are truly blessed to have you in our lives. Thank you from the bottom of our hearts.